The Handyman's Guide to the Galaxy

(Adventures in Professional Home Repair)

Justin Locke

978-0-9792901-1-4

www.justinlocke.com

Also by Justin Locke:

Real Men Don't Rehearse
(Adventures in the Secret World
of Professional Orchestras)

Principles of Applied Stupidity

Family concert works:

Peter VS. the Wolf

The Phantom of the Orchestra

Introduction

I never had any plans to be a handyman. I am not sure anyone ever does. While there are many late night TV ads for becoming a specialist in HVAC installation and repair, I have never seen an ad for a school that teaches you how to replace a broken window, replace three inches of missing bathroom grout, unstick a drawer in an antique dental cabinet, and while you're at it could you please look at where a squirrel got in the house and chewed up a baseboard?

As was the case with so many of my other "careers," I blindly stumbled into this one. It started when an electrician hired me to do some management consulting. Every day I watched him with envy and amazement. Unlike every other kind of work I have ever been involved in, for him, there was no need for the act of "selling." Instead, the phone just constantly rang off the hook all day, with calls from customers old and new, willing to pay whatever it cost to get the lights back on.

One day I casually mentioned to one of the electrician's clients that I was thinking of becoming a handyman.

Without missing a beat, she asked, "What are you doing Monday?"

And that's how it started. It was a little bit like learning how to swim by falling overboard, but I managed.

At that point, I did possess some general fixit skills. I have always been a "handy guy." Over the years I have painted my apartments and refinished old furniture for fun. But that is a far cry from doing this sort of thing for other people, for money.

So this book is really about a journey of discovery. It's not so much about being a handyman as it is about the process of *becoming* a handyman. It's very much about confronting new puzzles on a daily basis, and dealing with odd conventions and traditions. It's also about doing, not just a quick fix, but a fix that will stand the test of time.

As my electrician client used to say,

"It's a learning curve."

8

A Day in the Life

I had just spent four hours working on nice suburban home
outside of Boston. (In this case, I had replaced a broken sash
cord on an old wooden window.) As I was loading my car, a
little old lady–who had to be 95 at least–came up to me on the
street. She asked if I was a handyman. I said, absolutely.

Now, a little handyman algebra for you:

 Upscale neighborhood
+ Big old 1920's era Victorian house
+Rich little old lady

   = ka *ching*.

Not always, but often enough.

"She then asked, "Would mind just coming inside to take a
look at a few things?" I said, "Sure," and in we went.

Three steps in, and she opened a door to a small half-bathroom
off the kitchen, and there . . . was a ceiling light fixture.

It was a regular old metal fixture base, housing a single
incandescent bulb, surrounded by a big glass globe. The globe

was larger than average, maybe a little bigger than a basketball.

There was nothing unusual about this. Old houses often have these light fixtures that have fairly ornate, antique glass globes around them.

But what WAS unusual here was that this globe–a large hollow glass ball that housed a working, energized, brightly glowing, electric light bulb–was half filled . . .

. . . with water.

Actually, I just assumed it was water. Potential big mistake there. In retrospect, it could have been gasoline or acetone. When you work as a handyman, you learn that anything is possible, no matter how unlikely or insane it might seem. Fortunately, at this point the lady of the house interjected that she had had some sort of plumbing leak issue in the bathroom above, and that, in her opinion, had led to this water filled globe hanging overhead. Still, you can never be absolutely sure about these things.

Most people immediately panic when they hear the word "water" next to the word "electricity." And, well . . . they should. It's generally not a good idea to mix water and electricity. Especially not in a big fragile glass container suspended right over one's head, hanging on a fixture base that may or may not have been installed correctly, and even if it HAD been installed correctly, it was probably done in 1938 . . . and who knows what squirrels or silverfish may have been gnawing on the connections or screw holes in the meantime. Again, I don't mean to sound overly paranoid or mistrustful of my fellow human beings, but I have learned it pays to be cautious. You just never know.

Before you panic too much about the electricity mixed with water, here is a little handyman trivia for you: it is actually very common for light fixtures to get wet. Ice dams, broken pipes, and second floor bathtubs can spew water all over everything, and if water comes cascading down from the attic into your light fixtures, well, the bulbs may explode and the circuit breakers may trip, but all is not lost. Once all the water drains out and it all gets dry again, the fixtures, and their wires, generally speaking, will work just fine. No permanent damage. Not that I'm guaranteeing anything.

Along with the proximity of water to an energized circuit, in this rather extreme case, there were other issues to be considered: first was the sheer weight of the thing. A gallon of water weighs about eight pounds, and so this massive glass globe (of unknown structural integrity, as again, it was probably hand blown in 1938 and had been hanging there ever since) probably had about fifteen or twenty pounds of water sloshing around in it– plus the original weight of the glass globe itself. . . all this, suspended from a live light fixture that was installed by a guy who has probably been dead since 1968. Hmmm.

Now at this point, given all this information, you might pop up and say, "Well that's great, just turn off the power to the light by flicking off the switch, and go at it." And you might be right. Then again . . .

A quick lesson in electrical circuits: simply stated, in a basic circuit, you have two wires coming up from the fuse box in the basement: one is the "hot" wire, the other is the "neutral" wire.

As you may have guessed, the electrical power is in the HOT wire. In a standard simple light switch, the power in the hot wire comes up from the basement into the switch. The switch acts as a dam, interrupting the circuit, stopping the flow of power to the light fixture.

If that is the setup, great, turning off the switch will completely kill the power to the light fixture, making it totally dead and safe.

BUT

BUT

Just because the switch on the wall is off, that does not mean the power in the fixture is off.

For example, sometimes, the power is NOT coming up from the fuse box in the basement into the switch. Instead, when they built the house, the nearest source of power for this light fixture might have been an outlet on the floor above. If so, the guy who installed the light fixture back in 1938 may have cut a corner by running the hot wire straight from that outlet into the fixture first, and then running the circuit's wires down to the switch second. The switch will still operate the light, but this creates something called a neutral switch. It's a very naughty code violation, but sometimes people do things they are not supposed to because they don't know they aren't supposed to. Hey, the light works.

If the hot wire has in fact been fed directly into the fixture FIRST, that means, with wall switch on or wall switch off, the potential power of the hot wire (i.e., 110 volts) is still up in that fixture, just waiting for a chance to travel somewhere. It means that if you were to touch the ceiling light fixture the wrong way and then touch another path to ground like a metal ladder or a water pipe at the same time . . .   Uh oh.

BZZZZHHHT   Some portion of your epidermis is now a puff of blue smoke. Ouch. Might even kill you. In any case, you would be really really sorry you didn't call a licensed electrician.

There are other possible scenarios, but the point I am making here is, just because the switch is off, that does not mean there is no power in the box above the fixture. If you were to get a shock, and that shock hit you while you were holding an antique glass globe of unknown *Antiques Roadshow* valuation, filled with 20 pounds of water sloshing about thus making it even more unstable in your hand (and again, we are merely assuming it is water), well, . . . you get the idea. And those are just the dangers we know about. Who knows if termites have eaten through the floor below or above? Anything is possible. Those Farmers Insurance ads ain't got nuthin' on me.

That said, I figured I needed to do SOMETHING, as leaving a water-filled 20 pound glass ball suspended overhead with 110 volts of electricity hooked up to it . . . would be criminally negligent. So, up on a step stool.

Feeling around, I found the standard 3 little screws under the "lip" of the glass globe. These were all that stood between the head of any person sitting on the toilet beneath and an explosion of glass and water thereupon (again, we *hope* it's water). Whilst balancing on this little inverted bucket that claimed to be a step stool, and carefully supporting the 20 pounds of water-filled antique glass, I carefully (and I do mean carefully) unscrewed the 3 little screws, all of which, by the way, were rusty and hanging in there by their 80-year-old threads. Once they were undone, I brought the globe to my chest and carefully stepped off the step stool.
With a feeling similar to that of having just diffused a bomb, I

took this globe over to the sink, emptied it out, and cleaned it out. At the lady's request I put it back up where it was. It only occurred to me afterwards that the leak from upstairs, the one that had originally filled this thing with water in the first place, might not have been fixed, in which case the whole process may repeat . . . but she never called me again, thank God.

Just as a side note, I took a quick look around, and in this whole massive beautiful $2 million house, there were no smoke or CO detectors. I offered to come back and put some in but I never heard back from her.

The things you see.

If You Worked on it Before

A handyman's perception of the world tends to be somewhat skewed. Just as a doctor lives in a world populated by people who are sick and injured, a handyman lives in a world filled with broken stuff. Much of the broken stuff I see is the result of time and use; things break simply because they are old and worn out. That in itself is an endless pipeline of jobs. But on top of the work provided by Father Time, much of the business of the handyman world is created by ignorance. Before I cast any more stones, let me start by confessing some of my own many sins in this department.

This whole handyman thing started ages ago, when I was in my 20's. I moved into an apartment which was the upstairs of a huge two-family built in 1920.

The landlord was a great guy, but he had no interest in being a landlord, that is, he had no skills at, nor any interest in, house maintenance. Ordinarily this might be a problem for a tenant, but this landlord had one overwhelmingly redeeming feature:

He never raised the rent.

As I stayed for more and more years in this vast apartment (that I was eventually paying less than half market rate for), it became increasingly clear to me which side my butt was breaded upon. If anything went wrong with this old house, I did not even think of calling the landlord. I dealt with it myself. I did this for 20 years, starting with virtually no knowledge or experience.

Just one example of extreme wrongdoing on my part:

The building had no laundry facilities. After a few years of putting up with this, someone sold me a washer and a dryer for cheap, and I moved them into my half of the basement. (Yes,, I had half of the basement for storage, also the entire attic. I hope you are seeing why I was so happy to be my own landlord.) Out of my own pocket, I paid a plumber and an electrician to install the needed hookups, and hooray, I was finally in a house with laundry facilities.

But what I did not know, and there was no one around to tell me this, was that clothes dryers . . . need to be vented. Oh sure, I know that now, but, this being my first clothes dryer, I did not know it then. I DID tend to notice that when I ran the dryer, the basement would seem awfully humid. And I actually did ask someone at a hardware store about this, and they sold me a device that claimed it would fix the issue: It was a dryer vent doodad that directed the lint-laden humid air into a water filled bucket.

Theoretically, the water in the bucket would catch the flying lint. Of course, I was supposed to empty and re fill the bucket with every wash, and I kind of sort of forgot about that—not that it really mattered, as such devices don't do anything to prevent all the moist air being vented into the basement. I just did not know any better.

Over the years, this dryer just dumped its lint laden damp air into this basement, probably causing some mold as well as fouling the fuel jets in the oil furnaces. I was totally ignorant, but my clothes were getting washed, so I did not think about it any further. I eventually moved out, and that is the end of the story.

In the major trades like plumbing and electrical, there are training systems in place, like apprenticeships and certifications. These systems are there to make sure that people who work in those trades know how to do things properly. But in the more sketchy realms of handymen, or homeowners doing house maintenance, the element of caveat emptor becomes ever more magnified. There are no licenses required for installing storm doors, nor are there any city inspectors for down spouts, so anyone can do these installations any way they like.

If you hear me moaning in future chapters about some of the things I encounter in this line of work, well, bear in mind, it's not directed at the people who are ignorant; the frustration is with the all too common ignorance itself, and all the ensuing damage it causes.

When you come across a bad installation, it's a little like examining a crime scene. At a crime scene, all you may have is a dead body and some broken glass, and you have to search for clues as to how it all happened, so you can apprehend the murderer.

In the realm of handyman work, it's not so much about apprehending the offender, as it was usually someone who didn't know any better and is now long gone, so that's a lost cause . . . but many times, in order to undo what they did wrong, first you have to figure out just exactly WHAT they did wrong, and why, so you can fix the problem. And sometimes there was both an original problem and their incorrect fix overlaid on top of it. So now you have two problems to remedy.

But even ignorance is not entirely random. It often occurs in patterns. One kind of ignorant fix is what I call the "had it in the truck" fix. For example, sometimes you might come across a problem that is a very simple fix but it requires a special kind of screw, metal plate, or tube of sticky goop. All you have to do is run to the local hardware store, get the proper part, and put it in. But of course, running to the hardware store takes time, and so a large number of improper fixes are there because someone had something kinda sorta close to the needed part in their truck, and just used that instead of the proper fix. Granted, this is sometimes motivated by cheapness, but then again, it's quite likely they did not know there was a better fix.

A similar sort of problem is what I call the "pragmatic short term" fix. My dryer vent issue was a perfect example of that. Once I could run a load of wash, I had achieved my immediate goal, so I was done. I did not stop to think about any long term consequences.

Here is a simplified hypothetical example of a pragmatic short term fix: Let's say you have a hole in an exterior wall of a house. The pragmatic short term fix is to take a small board, cover the hole with it, and attach it with a nail. The hole is covered, problem solved.

But this approach fails to take into account what may happen in six months. Most people do not have extensive first hand experience with rotted wood, so they may lack awareness of the need to take steps to avoid it.

When the board gets wet, it will warp then start to rot; and then it might rot in such a way that the rot, or ants or termites, will leap into the rest of the house; or it may catch rainwater in an odd way that attracts centipedes or causes mold; or the nail might rust and make a brown streak down the side of the house. Alas, most of us have to learn about rotten wood the hard way, two years after the fact.

Another example, again taken from my fabulous huge cheap apartment with the moldy basement: the previous owners had felt a need for an additional outlet in a dining room. Instead of calling an electrician and doing it properly, they just plugged an extension cord into one outlet, stapled the extension cord onto the top of the baseboard, cut a hole in the wall on the other side of the room for another outlet, and then ran the extension cord wire around the faceplate. They cut off the end of the extension cord, and attached its wires to the back of the new outlet.

Now again, it was a pragmatic short term fix, and I am sure the lamp they plugged into this homemade outlet worked fine. And it probably kept them from tripping on an extension cord wire. But what if, years later, someone like me went to this ersatz outlet and plugged in a space heater or a window air conditioner? The extension cord was not designed to carry that much power, nor was it grounded. Or worse, what if a toddler yanked on the cord, and pulled the exposed end of energized wires off their little tiny screws? Again, at its inception, it was a nifty, clever, short term pragmatic fix, but oh my, it is so easy to just see the immediate goal and not stop to think about the many unfortunate things that might happen. It is usually ignorance, not malfeasance, but it's still just as dangerous.

Sometimes you will see a basement in an old house where not

one, but 15 or more pragmatic short terms fixes have been constructed over time. Someone wanted some power over here, so they spliced some wire into an outlet, ran the wire across the dirt floor, and powered something else. It works fine until someone trips on the wire, or you have a flood, at which point you learn the hard way why we have electrical code rules. It astonishes me that people with basements like this can get fire insurance.

Wherefore Art Thou, Poka-Yoke

I suppose I should not get too upset at ignorance in action, because down the line I do make a fair amount of money from it. Just an example of the latter:

One day a regular client called me up. Her problem was, she had ordered some end tables from one of those "assemble-it-yourself" furniture companies. Upon its arrival, someone, a relative or a neighbor or whatever, had jumped up and said "Oh yeah, I can out that together for you."

He got about half way through the process, when . . . uh oh. Clearly something was not right. The little drawers would not fit at all. At that point he got totally lost and confused, and disappeared.

Now again, returning to our ignorance theme, there is primary level of ignorance, which is simply that which we don't know, and then there is a very nasty subset of ignorance, which is not knowing what we don't know. If we think we know something, we can't help but feel a sense of status and pride. But when we are confronted with hard proof that we don't know as much as we thought we did, this can be an embarrassing shock to the system. This is why humility is so important, in both life and in handymanning. It lessens the shock. Confidence is of course key, but when it is not tempered by humility, it can be your downfall, as it was in this guy's case.

The makers of these assemble-it-yourself products always try to emphasize the ease and simplicity of the assembly process. Alas, if you believe anything that says "easy," that's a trap waiting for the uninitiated. Only because I have personally done so many of these beastly things do I know how VERY easy it is to get lost, and screw things up by putting something in backwards. With experience comes humility and caution.

In dealing with this half assembled end table, I was reminded of those joke signs, usually posted in gas station garages, that say

"Labor– $70 an hour
If you watch– $80/hr
If you help – $100 an hour
If you worked on it already – $120 an hour."

The last line seemed to apply well in this case, as I had to study this thing for 20 minutes to try and see what was wrong. Eventually I discovered that the "runners"– the metal strips that held the drawers in place–had been installed either backwards, or upside down, or both.

There is a nifty methodology in the manufacturing philosophy of the Toyota Company known as "poka-yoke." This term means "mistake- proofing." To give you an example, if there is a small electrical plug in a Toyota Prius, they will make the plug in such a way that's it's pretty much impossible for the guy on the assembly line to accidentally install it backwards or upside down. Some little pin will be sticking out to prevent the error. But alas, most assemble-it-yourself furniture has no such safeguards, and you must study the instructions very carefully. Otherwise, you can easily put something in upside down, and not discover your error until you have installed six other pieces on top of it . . . which is basically what this other person had done.

I disassembled the thing bit by bit, going in reverse in the sequence of directions (directions that, by the way, were close to impossible to read going forwards). After much trial and error, I finally came to a point in the assembly process where everything matched the directions and everything that had been done wrong had been undone. At least, I had about an 80% certainty, which, in handymanning, are pretty good odds. I ultimately succeeded, but at such cost, as ignorance had struck again.

What Rock through Yonder Window Breaks

Speaking of ignorant predecessors, one day a new client asked me to come look at her house problems. Like every other homeowner, she had accumulated a "list."

At the top of the list was a window that her brother-in-law or ex-boyfriend or whoever had tried to fix. It was a standard small window, divided into six small windows on each sash.

One of the six little windows had broken, so this guy had decided to take the entire window completely apart, and take it all out of the frame in the wall. Having done that, he then took the entire lower sash down to the hardware store to have them replace the one little broken square of glass.

Okay, this approach kinda, sorta made sense; HOWEVER . . . this window was on the first floor, facing a deck, so there was really no need to take the whole thing apart. All that was needed was to stand comfortably on the deck in the soft breeze and sunshine, and replace the broken window, which was about five feet off the ground. But . . . and alas, ignorance struck again. Since he did not know how to replace a broken window (and again, I admit to having been this ignorant on other projects myself, and still am at many things, so I can't be too critical) he decided to take the whole thing apart. I mean everything. Not just the sashes. The sash, the counterweight system, much of the frame . . . everything.

Handyman Rule #1: Taking things apart is generally a whole lot easier than putting them back together again.

While this person had done a totally wrong unnecessary disassembly, I admit, this DID have the plus factor of creating an opportunity for added billable hours for myself, so I could not be too upset with him. However, I did have mixed emotions:

You see, this was not a standard window. It was some kind of crazed experimental one-of-a-kind window, probably imported from Yugoslavia, that had a system of spring-loaded counterweights, the likes of which I have never seen before or since. It took an hour to just decipher the thing and how it worked. And even then, it was mostly a lucky guess.

It was nasty, because the four spring-loaded pieces all had to be compressed at the same time in order to reload it back into the frame. It took about 25 failed attempts (each time with something going "SPROING" and my having to pull it out and start over) before I got it back in the frame in working condition.

That was bad enough, but it gets worse: this window was in a small office that had a built-in desk all around the edges of this tiny room, so I had to kneel on the top of this desk while holding all the pieces of this window. All in all it took about three hours. Yeesh.

The Doors

One day a new customer called me up and said her front door was not closing right. She had called someone else to fix it, but apparently he had not done it right. (Are you cringing yet?)

Over I went, braced for what I would find . . . .

I confess to having a very bad mental habit: when people call up and describe a certain symptom, I allow myself to fantasize that this will be just a "simple fix" . . . and I gleefully drive over to the job, thinking I am going to make a minimum service call fee of one hour's work, while only having to work for five minutes. But even though I still catch myself indulging in this easy money fantasy, I can confidently tell you that this has never, ever, EVER proven to be the case. It is always, always, always more complicated and time consuming than I think it will be.

In this case, I had allowed myself to think that this door, that was not closing right, was the common case of the top hinge screws coming loose after 70 years of use. If that was the issue, all that would be is required is a few quick turns of a screwdriver, and magically the door would again close as it was designed to close 75 years ago. I would be done, I would be the hero, I would get paid, hooray.

Yeah, right.

Okay, so this elegant old house had what is called a "tongue in groove" door.

Tongue in groove was once a method of weatherstripping/ weatherproofing a door. If you don't know what tongue in groove weatherstripping is, well, the door itself has a teensy little trench/groove cut into it, all around, on the interior-facing side, about 3/4 of an inch from the edge.

Then, on the jamb (that's the sides, or the frame of the doorway) itself, going up both sides and across the top, there is a little 3/8 inch "tongue" of soft metal sticking out. When you close the door, that tiny "tongue" of metal fits ever so nicely into the "groove" that was cut in the door, thus making a reasonably air tight seal.

When I got there, the owner showed me how this magnificent old door was not closing all the way. It was closing mostly, but it really needed to go another ½ inch or so. As it was, it was slightly ajar, not closing enough to make the tongue fit into the groove, so the wind was whistling in.

Sad to say, before she called me, she had called someone else. She had shown him how the door was not closing all the way, thus she was not able to lock her door. Since door was not closing all the way, neither of the 2 deadbolts, nor the latch of the knob lock, were lining up with their respective "strike plate" holes in the door frame.

So again, the great bugaboo of ignorance:

Instead of figuring out why the door was not closing properly, this fellow accepted the state of the unclosed door, and moved on to what I admit was a very pragmatic fix. Instead of messing with the broken door, he proceeded to move all the strike plates, that is, he set to cutting out new holes in the jamb, where all the latches and deadbolts went into the door frame/jamb.

Ay caramba. This is some pretty serious chopping up of a door jamb, folks.

He took all the metal strike plates off, chiseled out larger holes ½ inch closer to the interior of the house, drilled more holes for all the screws, and put the strike plates back on, leaving gouged out holes all around everywhere.

Now I will admit . . . I will admit . . . when he was all done, you COULD in fact lock the door, albeit in a somewhat ajar /open position. Great. A classic pragmatic short term fix.

At this point, yes, you could turn the two deadbolt knobs, and the deadbolts would go into the strike plates, even though the door itself was still not fully closed. And this is what I saw when I arrived . . . along with all the gaping gashes of where the strikeplate holes used to be.

This was so sad. Doors are not rocket science.

Now I should be careful here because for all I know, what I proceeded to do next might, in some distant expert's eyes, be totally stupid and wrong. But, working at the best of my ability, I started by asking, WHY is this door not closing right? I took a quick look at the metal tongue, and sure enough, at the bottom, someone had kicked this tongue piece of metal and bent it.

These metal tongues are pretty soft by design, and right at the bottom, this little piece of metal tongue had been bent just enough to stop the door from closing. I took some needle nose pliers and bent this piece of door tongue back into position–which took me all of 25 seconds–and now the door was closing all the way again. Hooray.

Only problem was, the strike plates had all been moved, so now, if you wanted to lock the door, you had to open it a half inch again. SOOOOO . . . the strike plates now all had to be moved back to their original locations, even though the jamb looked like a beaver convention had been in town last weekend.

It took all day, but I managed to get the strike plates back in proper position. I actually improved security by installing better strike plates with pockets for the deadbolts using four inch screws, then I filled in all the gouged out holes with wood filler. Once it was all sanded and painted, it looked like new, but oh my goodness, what a nightmare for the client and me.

Warp Speed

Speaking of ignorance:

One day a new client called me to come over to fix a door, fix a drawer, replace a doorknob, the usual "list." And then . . . she showed me her brand new deck.

At first glance, it looked like a standard deck. It had railings, it had steps, whatever. But as I looked more closely, it became obvious that all of the boards that made up the surface of this deck—had warped. Each long board was a gully, with the edges higher than the middle. It was really weird trying to walk on this distorted, anything-but-flat surface.

Looking around further, it also became obvious that all the many hundreds of hails that had been used to construct this deck . . . were rusting away.

I am not a construction guy, and I know nothing about building decks, so I said very little at the time. But this event sent me running home to Google, and to anyone I could find who had deck construction experience. I was just terribly curious.

What I quickly learned was, one cannot use any old kind of

wood for a deck. You have to use wood that can cope with being outside in the rain and snow. You can use wood from specific water-resistant species of tree, but the most common approach is to use something called "pressure treated lumber."

Pressure treated lumber is infused with chemicals that prevent water from seeping into the wood and causing it to warp. (It also makes the wood very unappetizing to wood-eating insects.) I also learned, when building a deck, that you have to use special rust resistant screws.

This particular crime scene was a bit of a puzzlement. The general carpentry work on this warped deck seemed to be pretty okay. So I was left wondering, how could someone with that much woodworking skill have made such a blatant error? Pressure treated lumber and rust resistant screws do cost a little more, but was that cost difference the motivating factor here? That seemed so unlikely, as the cost difference was so minor, especially when compared to the damage done, to both deck and reputation, by cutting such a vital corner. Perhaps there was a plan to seal up the wood after the fact.. Alas, my own ignorance is showing here. I will likely never know the whole story, but for the moment, I have to suspect that sheer ignorance had struck yet again.

Socket To Me

When you do handyman work, you start to see the physical world in a very different way.

Before doing this work for a living, I sailed through life with a certain childlike naïveté about the floors I walk on and the ceiling I walk under. But one of the first things you learn when working on the infrastructure of the world is that all of the people who design all these modern conveniences, both bridges and bathtubs, work within and around "tolerances."

In your tap water, you may have mercury and lead, and probably a little strontium 90, but as long as it's under some magic number, like, e.g., 10 ppb (parts per billion), it's "within tolerances." Things are never perfect; most things just work within their tolerances. You have to be mindful that there are always limits to how much weight, how much pressure, how many amps, how much heat, or how much cold, that a given screw, nail, hook, pipe, or wire can take before it fails. Ideally, things would never fail, but everything, including you and me, has a breaking point. And you just have to work within these very imperfect parameters.

For someone like me, with more than a little touch of OCD, this is just so terribly hard. You can never be absolutely positively sure about anything. One example is electricity and standard table lamps.

We have all heard horror stories of small children taking screwdrivers and sticking them into electrical outlets, and poodles being electrocuted by stepping on electrified manhole covers. But as horrifying as it is to think of someone sticking their finger into electrical socket, we all do something very similar, just 1/32 of an inch away from it, every time we turn on a table lamp.

If you look at the socket of a standard old table lamp, first, you'll see the socket, i.e., the big hole into which the bulb is screwed. On the side of the socket is a switch, usually either a little sliding rod, or a little knob that you twist. The sliding rod, especially, requires you to actually touch the socket itself. We all do this every day. No big deal, right?

Well, hidden inside that socket are two little screws, and on one of those screws, you attach the end of a wire that is hooked up directly to the electrical wall socket we were just so recently horrified by. And all that separates your fingers from that bare wire, a wire that is directly hooked up to 120 volts of electricity, is a very thin sleeve of cardboard.

That's it.

But amazingly, this system, however slight, works beautifully. That thin bit of cardboard is actually all the insulation you need.

After all, when you hold the power cord of a toaster or a vacuum cleaner while it is plugged in, that same amount of potential electrical shock is just a 16th of an inch away from you.

Trouble is, if someone were to rewire that table lamp and say to themselves "Hey, what do I need this stupid little piece of cardboard for?" and toss it aside, well, now they have opened the door to you doing your own version of sticking your finger into an electrical socket.

Hopefully, when you touch this equivalent of an energized wire, you are wearing tennis shoes and you're not touching a water pipe with your other hand. But if you are… BZZZHHHHT.

The potential hazards and traps of table lamps don't end there. If the lamp was rewired by someone who didn't know what they were doing, there are two other problems that can easily manifest. One is, they may have failed to tie an "underwriters knot." The other is reversed polarity.

If you are rewiring a lamp, you would start by running the wire into the bottom of the lamp and threading it up to the top. Once you thread the wire into the bottom of the socket, it is very important that you tie a special kind of knot called an "underwriter's knot" in the electrical wire. This keeps the wire from being accidentally pulled down and out of the socket.

If that knot is not there, and some kids or the dog knock the lamp over, the lack of an underwriter's knot might allow the wire to get pulled back out of the bottom of the lamp. If the lamp is still plugged in, you now have a bare energized wire staring you in the face, just waiting to cause all sorts of fire and mayhem.

And finally, the polarity pitfall:

The single wire of your table lamp is actually two wires stuck together. One is the hot, the other is the neutral. The hot goes to the gold screw on the socket, the neutral goes to the silver screw. It is very easy to get these two reversed. If this happens, the hot wire is no longer powering the gold contact point that is tucked way down in the bottom of the socket. Instead, it is energizing the silver threads, maybe even the brass socket itself, and worse than that, those threads are now energized 24/7 whether the switch is on or off. If this happens, it becomes that much more likely that you will get a nasty shock.

These are just a few things to think about when someone offers to rewire a lamp for you, or you pick one up at a yard sale.

Oh, and by the way, there is yet another pitfall awaiting. This occurs when you plug the lamp into the wall outlet.

When installing a wall outlet, it is very easy to get the wires crossed. If the person who installed the outlet made an error and wired the outlet in reverse, meaning, if the hot wire got connected to the neutral screw and the neutral wire got connected to the hot screw (and there is nothing to prevent this from happening other than the knowledge of the installer), well, even if the lamp is wired perfectly, you now have the same risk of shock from the lamp that you would have had with crossed wires in the socket.

Throne Room

There is one building I work on on a regular basis. It is the mortal remains of what was once a magnificent old house, but is now cut up into student housing. The current owner was not personally responsible for much of what is there, but it's amazing to see what the previous owners did. Where to begin?

To start, there are zoning laws in this area that limit how many rental units you can have in a given building. So, as near as we can piece it together, somebody was (illegally) renting out the basement space as an apartment of sorts. It must have been a pretty grim space to live in, but I am sure the price was right.

There was no evidence of a kitchen, (I think it has since been remade into the common laundry) but it did have a bathroom and a living room. Here was the catch: the only sewer pipe in the basement ran across the place at about two feet off the floor. This is common in basements, but the problem was, toilets generally work on gravity, i.e., once you flush it, there is no pump, it all just wants to go downhill to a sewage drain pipe that is below the toilet. But here, the only drain pipe available was 2 feet above the ground. What to do?

At this point, I have to bow to the cleverness, imagination, and sheer outside the litterbox thinking they displayed here. If the drain could not be put down, let's . . . lift the toilet up. They built a little three-foot-high platform right in the middle of this apartment, (as that was where this pipe was running), with a set of stairs leading up to it, and there they installed the toilet. Talk about sitting on the throne.

Code: It's More of a Rule than a Guideline

One day one of my regular clients called to tell me a story.

She had been out of town for a few weeks and someone had been house-sitting for her. One night a light bulb burned out, and the house sitter called an electrician to fix the problem (and no, I am not making that up). The electrician came out and changed the bulb. While they were doing this, they offered to do a free "26 point safety inspection."

Free stuff always sounds appealing, so the house-sitter let them go at it. A few weeks later, my client came home to find a note from the electrician. It listed $1100 worth of recommended fixes of "code violations."

Code violations? My house is in violation of code? Oh my God. Alert the media and call the fire department.

Well . . . not so fast. Let's not get our knickers in a twist just yet. Let's talk about codes. As in building codes.

Some people think of codes as an annoying overreach of governmental power, and sometimes I agree. But for the most part, building codes are a very good thing.

Bear in mind that I am NOT a licensed electrician (or licensed anything else), thus everything I say on the topic should be viewed with extreme suspicion. That said, let's suppose you have a basement, and you need to throw some light in a dark corner. Let's also assume that you are somewhat handy and clever, and also somewhat cheap. You could easily pop over to the hardware store and get a plug and some wire. You could then attach the wire to the plug, put the plug into a wall outlet, run that wire across a wet cement or dirt floor, run the wire up to a rafter, attach it with a nail or duct tape, use a coat hanger to hang an old fixture, screw in a 60 watt bulb, and voila, you would have light. A classic cheap quick pragmatic fix.

But the problem is, your production has not accounted for any dangers stemming from possible random future events. For example, someday, some kids or some dogs might get into the basement and start running around. There is now a considerable likelihood that the dangling wire you installed will come loose and zap somebody, or start a fire. This is why we have codes.

In this case, electrical code would have required that instead of just plugging into an outlet, the wire should be spliced into a wall outlet box, and securely attached therein. Then, when running the wire across the room, it would have to be securely attached to a joist, or otherwise held out of the way of general traffic. That way, if you were to move an armoire across the basement, there would be less of a chance of accidentally dislodging a dangling hot wire.

The fixture itself would have to be firmly attached to an electrical box, one that would also hold the wire securely, thus preventing any energized wires from being yanked out and falling into the sump pump. Also, any wire splice points would be contained in the box, so if perchance some sparks were to fly, they would be contained in the box. There would also be a ground wire in the mix.

Yes, you can quickly and cheaply run a wire in such a way to get light here or there, but that does not allow for the many worst case scenarios that might result. Improperly installed wires are far more vulnerable to being yanked or exposed in such a way that they could cause a fire, or shock someone walking past. Are we understanding code yet?

One of the most common code violations I encounter is the absence of a proper box above a ceiling light fixture. This is not just individual homeowners doing this. I have seen full-fledged building contractors cut this corner. It seems like once a month someone will ask me to replace a malfunctioning ceiling light, I will pull it down, and lo and behold, there is no ceiling light box. Instead, there will just be a little plate fastened to a flammable wooden joist, and the wire connections will be casually shoved up against the ceiling. (When I encounter such situations, I just stabilize everything as best I can, back away, and tell the client to call an electrician.)

Now granted, being a cheapskate myself, I can see their argument. Ceilings are usually made of either plaster or drywall and generally are not very flammable, even if they heat up. But then again– what if someone walks through the attic, trips on the loose wire, and yanks the hot wire out of the light? Now you have an energized wire hanging about loose just looking for trouble. Also, most light fixtures will have a sticker telling you to not use bulbs over 60 watts, but what if someone does not read that, and puts in 100 watt bulbs? Now you have a dangerously high concentration of heat in the fixture, and if there is no box, that heat is now being transferred directly to a flammable wooden joist. Eventually, it might start to smoke. When people ignore code, it invites disaster.

Also, any time you have electrical wires spiced together, you have a potential for sparks if things come loose. But as long as the sparks are properly confined in their box, nothing much else is likely to happen, because even if there is flammable pile of old sheet music nearby, the sparks will be contained in the box. And if a spider crawls into the box and lays eggs month after month, building up flammable material, well, even if the eggs catch on fire, it will all stay within the box. Are you getting why we have code now?

I have a client who has an old house with some outdoor motion sensor lights. Whoever installed these lights ignored code. They just ran some wire through an outside wall, and spliced the wires onto the motion light fixture connections. The lights work great, but there is no box holding the wire splices. They are right out in the open on top of this light fixture. Granted, it's all under a porch roof, so it's not likely to get wet, but what if . . . what if . . . some enterprising sparrow decides to build a nest on this oh-so-appealing spot (as it is slightly warmer at night due to the energized wires)? Now you have two spliced electrical wires sitting right underneath a pile of bird's nest kindling . . . right next to the house. Are we understanding the purpose of code yet?

Back to my original client story of supposedly $1100 worth of massive code violations:

Yes, my client did have multiple code violations in her house, but most of them were simply the lack of GFCI outlets. And now, dear friends, we get into a grey area.

GFCI (a.k.a. ground fault circuit interrupt) outlets are designed to shut down if they notice a sizeable leap in how much power is going through them. If you don't have these in your bathroom, here is the issue: if you are making toast in your bathroom while someone is in the tub, and you toss the toaster into the tub, you might kill the person in said tub. On the other hand, if the toaster is plugged into a GFCI outlet, the outlet will sense the sudden jump in current, and it will shut itself off before your friend in the tub can get fully zapped.

But in this client's case, all of her kids were grown up and long gone, so no one used that guest bathroom any more. So do you really need to install a GFCI?

Never let it be said that I ever told anyone to ignore a building code. And yes, "code requires" GFCI outlets in all potentially wet areas like basements, garages, bathrooms, and kitchens. But will you be fined by the city for these violations? Not likely. Will these minor code violations prevent you from selling your house? Probably not. Will a man with a gun come round and arrest you? I doubt it. To me, the biggest code violation here was the unnecessary panicking of a naïve homeowner for the purpose of drumming up more business.

Someday, when my client goes to sell her house, these items might become a point of contention, depending on the pickiness of the home inspector. But the place where codes really come into play is in new construction.

If you build a brand new addition on your house, or if you remodel the kitchen, or perhaps replace a staircase, yes, a man from the city will come and require you and your new addition to follow code to the letter. But in an existing old house (and remember, I am not a lawyer so please do not rely upon this), minor things that were legal when the house was built are generally tolerated by the powers that be until the day when you do a complete remodel. Yes, it's always a good idea to bring things up to code in an old house if you can, but let's not panic about it.

Bear in mind, we haven't even begun to touch on other code issues like plumbing or staircase code. In really old houses, there are so many code violations, you can't bring them fully up to code without tearing them down and starting all over again. So, you use common sense.

Winging It

There is one aspect of handymanning that can get rather intense, and that is the experience of "on the spot" problem solving. This is one of the most nerve racking, and occasionally also one of the most rewarding, aspects of the work.

A little consumer advice: whenever you contact a fixit person with a problem or a project, please do not assume that your problem is a common issue. Instead, assume it is the first such problem that has ever occurred since the dawn of time. Send a picture of the offending door, window, fence, hinge, tree, wall, whatever. Handymen are only human, and we want to be as prepped as we can be to address your issue.

On a more pragmatic level, most tradespeople just want to get in and get out. If we come to your house and encounter something unexpected and unfamiliar, it's awkward. We are supposed to be experts. We don't like to look stupid and confused in front of customers. We don't want to call Honeywell Help and be kept on hold for 10 minutes with you staring at us.

I was doing some basic paint and door fix work in a beautiful old house for a lovely retired couple, and as I was completing "the list," I asked, "What else ya got?" And it's funny, sometimes people have become unconscious of issues because they have been living with them for so long. After a long pause, the lady of the house directed my attention to a kitchen drawer. Her body language clearly implied "I don't expect that you can do anything about this but . . ."

This was not the original-to-the-house ancient drawer I was expecting. It was a basic modern kitchen drawer, with the little white nylon wheels all around. It seemed to have been installed recently as part of an overall kitchen remodel. When I pulled it out, it more or less worked, but it made a noise, KA CHUCK, and then once it had gone half way, it went BANG. At various points in its travels from closed to open it would bind a little, then it would actually rock up and down like a teeter totter. And when you closed it, it would make the exact same noises and have the exact same binding feel, only in reverse.

Okayyyyyyyyy . . . This sure ain't right. But at this point in my handymanning career, while I had become a glowing expert in all things door and window, I had never done any work on a modern drawer with wheels and runners. Public speaking may be people's number one fear, but trying to fix something you have never seen before, on the spot, while people are watching, is a pretty close second.

I should have backed away and run home to YouTube, but I have this problem: I get target fascinated with seemingly simple devices that do not work. So, whilst the meter was running, and I was the object of the innocent, touching, childlike faith of these two clients looking at me like I was a medicine man with magical powers, I sat there looking at this drawer. I pulled it out and pushed it in, I pulled it out and pushed it in, and every single time, that drawer made the exact same KA CHUCK BANG noise with the exact same odd feel, like it was a teeter totter instead of a smooth slide.

One skill you must possess in this line of work is the ability think openly and ponder all sorts of odd possibilities. So as I was staring at this thing, I suddenly realized that there was a virtually identical drawer just below it, and THAT drawer was working perfectly. AHA. We have a reference for correct function. HOW IS THIS BROKEN UPPER DRAWER DIFFERENT FROM THIS LOWER DRAWER?

I confess I must have looked pretty silly sitting there on their kitchen floor opening and closing these drawers for I don't know how long, trying to see patterns, and differences in those patterns. Finally, I saw it. The left wheel/roller of the offending drawer was falling out of the runner track, but only at the end, when it was almost fully closed.

With a standard modern drawer design, inside the cabinet you have a "runner" which is just a two foot long, two inch wide piece of metal with a tiny quarter-inch lip of metal sticking out on both its top and its bottom. The wheel in the drawer runs along the lower lip of the runner, and the top lip keeps the drawer from falling down when pulled out.

But in this case, in the back of the cabinet, the runner itself was about an eighth of an inch too far away from the drawer. (I could only know this because of having the "correct" reference of the lower drawer.)

Clearly, I needed to somehow shim the runner out another eighth of an inch from the cabinet wall, NOT TOO FAR, and that SHOULD make the thing work right. And now I was in the land of uncertainty and drilling holes in someone's home, with the devout hope that my envisioned fix would in fact solve the problem without creating another one.

There was another giveaway here: someone had attempted to correct the issue by shimming the runner out a little with a piece of cardboard, but it was nowhere near thick enough. So obviously, they KNEW, but they had given up before making it right. Now I was even more contemptuous of their work. This was actually a good thing, because now I was feeling much more comfortable with mucking around with it.

I loosened the screws holding the runner. Then I took some shims and carefully put them under the runner, thus moving it over closer to the drawer. The whole time I was working inside a small drawer space doing "handyman yoga": I was in a very awkward position, working purely by eye and feel to get the distances right– we're talking an eighth of an inch adjustment. Moving it too far over would make it worse than the current problem.

There is an odd thing about this work: sometimes your savant subconscious kicks in, and you just magically get it right the first time, doing it purely by feel and guess work.

There is yet another bit of magic in this work. It is the moment where you have just executed what you believe to be the fix, but there is no knowing if your fix has worked until you test it. Many is the time when a good faith effort is completed and the test does NOT work.

After all that shimming on the runner, I replaced the drawer, and with all fingers crossed, I pushed it in, and . . . VIOLA . . . It rolled in just smooth and perfect.

Seems like a small thing I guess, but there is a fabulous rush of relief and smug pride when that happens. And of course the clients, who had been helplessly living with this drawer version of a pebble in their shoe for 10 years, just looked so amazed and grateful. It was a small and simple yet wonderful thing.

So You Want to Be a Handyman

For those of you out there with inquiring minds, you might be asking yourself, just how the heck does someone become a handyman? After all, there are no handyman universities out there, and precious few guidance counselors recommend it as a career path.

There is no real answer to that. It's very much a learn-by-doing situation, usually driven by chance, odd circumstance, and response to infinitely variable customer need.

Peter Drucker once said the purpose of a business is to create a customer, meaning, the purpose of business is to present a product or service to people that, once they are aware of it, they instantly have to have it. And if you say out loud in public that you are a handyman, or even just say you are *thinking of becoming* a handyman, you will create customers. Pete would be proud.

But even if you have customers, you still have to have SOME skills, so where do those come from? Well, here is one real life example:

Over the course of my first year of handymanning, a regular customer had asked me if I did vinyl siding repairs. I told her that I had never done that, but I was willing to give it a go. She said, "Well, this is a condo association thing so we need an estimate, etc.," and since I had no idea of how to do it or what it would cost, we just tabled the discussion. And it had always bugged me that 1) I had not met a customer need and 2) I had not made the money.

So even though that particular job faded into oblivion, this sent me running to YouTube to get a lesson in vinyl siding repair. And sure enough, there was a *This Old House* video on the whole process.

Whenever I am asked to do a job I have never done before, I have a very simple technique for knowing if I should do it or not: I go to YouTube, and if the only person telling me how to do something is Tommy on *This Old House*, and no one else on YouTube has posted a similar how-to video, I know it's too hard for me to do. And if Tommy and the gang called in a specialist to do the job instead of doing it themselves, ok, now we know it's absolutely beyond me, so forget it.

On the other hand, if there are at least seven other people posting how-to videos for the exact same problem/project, I know it is within my range.

So, as I had done at least 500 times before and 500 times since, I watched every video I could find on vinyl siding repair. And it all seemed eminently do-able. Of course, there is a massive difference between watching a video on something and actually doing it yourself. There is always a gremlin, i.e., some little trap hidden in the process that gets glossed over or completely left out that you have to figure out on the spot, as you will soon see.

A year of other projects went by and then lo and behold, a

50

brand new client walks in the e-door and asks if I can fix a small bit of damage in her vinyl siding. I said to her, "I will make you a deal: the job is not all that hard, I know how to do it in the abstract, but, full disclosure, I have never done it myself personally. That said, I would like to get some actual hands-on experience doing this job and add it to my repertoire, so how about I give you a bargain basement flat rate price for the job? That way you will get it done slow but cheap, and at the end I will know how to install vinyl siding fixes. Deal?" Of course she leapt at it.

Okay, so, vinyl siding fixes. How does that work? Well, step one is search on YouTube for video tutorials. Having done that already, the next step is getting the replacement piece. And this, my friends, is the beginning of true enlightenment.

I think it is safe to say that, while possessing the tools and skills needed to actually do the job is essential, perhaps 60% of many repair jobs is primarily about the research and getting the right parts and chemicals needed for the job.

I am often envious of people who do whole new remodeling projects or new construction, as they can just saunter down the aisle at Lowe's or Home Depot and freely pick and choose drywall, tile, paint, stone, and . . . vinyl siding.

On the other side of the screwdriver, when you are being asked to make a small patch on something that was installed 15 years ago and has been out in the sun and snow ever since, again, 60% of the job is finding materials that match the existing. Sometimes, like a doorknob, it's an obvious easy peasy remove-and-replace task. But anytime you are talking about matching the COLOR . . . Yikes. Welcome to the land of the lost.

When *This Old House* did their vinyl siding repair video, all Tommy said was "First you go to the supply house and get a replacement piece." Much as I love *This Old House*, in my humble opinion, that one was a bit of a dodge. Getting the replacement piece is the hardest part of the job. At least it was for me.

So, again, if you want to learn how to do this stuff, unless you have someone mentoring and training you, you have to do it all by trial and error. You just charge in, and start trial-ing and error-ing. This process can be a serious test of your character and fortitude. It's also a test of how much faith you have in your ability to solve unanticipated problems, especially those problems that occur after you have taken the thing down and cut it up and thus have passed the point of no return.

Now I will confess to you that at this point, in my total ignorance, I had made an assumption. (Incidentally, that is death for a handyman, to make assumptions about anything.)

In this case, knowing nothing about vinyl siding, I had assumed that all vinyl siding was the same in terms of its overall construction (after all, isn't that the way it SHOULD be done in a perfect world?). I figured all I needed to do was to find a piece of new siding that was the same color. So I went over to the client's house, climbed up on a ladder, and cut off a chunk of siding with my tin snips. (Vinyl siding is not easy to cut, but it's doable with some effort.)

Since Tommy on *This Old House* had said so casually that all I had to do was "go to the supply house and get a replacement piece," I also assumed that any big box hardware store would be the place to buy it. Again, assumptions, death for the handyman.

Off I went. There was no one around in the vinyl siding area (they DID sell vinyl siding, just in white, no colors) so I went up to their "pro desk" to seek advice and guidance.

To their credit, a very nice person at the pro desk looked at my jagged little piece of siding and pulled out some siding sample books. And we proceeded to look through the book to find a match.

We flipped through all these sample books, looking at pieces of siding that had all these fancy names. My chunk of siding was kinda pink-ish / peach-ish, so we considered "Prairie Sunrise" . . . "Summer Rose" . . . "Peach Harvest" . . . "River Pebbles," . . . and " Sand Dune" . . . (as I read all those wistful evocative names of these colors, I couldn't help but wonder who it is that sits in a cubicle somewhere making these things up, and do they make minimum wage, or 200 grand a year?)

We found a few samples that were close in color, but nothing really matching. After 45 minutes of this frustrating fruitless searching, I scribbled down the names of the various vinyl siding manufacturers that were printed on the back of the swatch books, and gave up for the day.

Are you learning yet? Are you exhausted? Oh, come now. Why, our little party's just beginning.

Next day I called the customer service number of one of these vinyl siding manufacturers. I was all set to email them a picture of the closest color in the swatch book and a picture of my jagged sample piece of siding. A very nice lady answered the phone. I told her my story, and she asked, "What is the number of the siding you have?"

Dead dumbfounded silence from me. Then I said:

"There's a number?"

"Yes," she said, "every piece of vinyl siding has a number printed on it. Just give me that number and we can get you a matching piece if we make it, or send you to the company that does make it.

DUH.

BACK TO THE CLIENT HOUSE WE GO

Now that we have learned to not bother to take cut-off bits of siding to a big box hardware store to get a replacement piece, we have a whole new skill you have to learn, i.e., how to remove vinyl siding in such a way that you can put it right back.

(There is another handyman skill you must master, which is, no matter what you are doing and no matter how simple it may seem, you must always think like a spy breaking into a safe and copying the enemy's codebook, being very careful not to touch or damage anything other than what you are directly working on, because if you break something else, you have to fix it for free, and your insurance has a $500 deductible. To continue:)

To remove vinyl siding, there is a special tool called a "zip" tool. They sell it at any hardware store. You take this little hand tool and you jam it up under the vinyl siding.

The process is eerily reminiscent of that scene from "Total Recall" where Arnold Schwarzenegger pulls the golf ball out of his nose. You shove the unfamiliar tool way way up, further than you really think you should, and once you think you have a grip on the bottom hook edge of the siding (each course of piece of siding overlaps the next, so you have to shove up about 4 inches), you pull down ... And you really don't feel good about this, as you have to pull down so hard it feels like you are sure to break the vinyl, but amazingly, at least in my case, the vinyl did not break, it held together, and once you have a grip, you essentially force the vinyl slat to come unhooked from the piece below it. Then you "zip" the tool along the bottom of the panel and it magically comes off for you.

Of course, you don't want to unzip any more of the siding panel than you absolutely have to, because whatever siding you unzip needs to be rezipped . . . And it has to be rezipped by you. And when you're doing something like this for the first time, and you don't really know what you're doing, one tends to default to the most conservative approach possible.

I unzipped about two feet of vinyl siding, and lo and behold, there was a little seven digit number printed on it. YAY.

I wrote down the number, I even took a picture of it as a backup, I took the two feet of vinyl that I had just recently unzipped and re zipped it, climbed down, put the ladder back in the car, and drove back home. Feeling terribly smug and superior that I now knew about numbers and that I had actually found the number, I called the manufacturer's customer service line one more time, and proudly recited the seven digit number to them.

I eagerly awaited a congratulatory comment of some sort, as well as the reasonably obsequious statement about how "I will go look that up for you." But instead, all I got was

A lengthy awkward silence.
Finally the woman said, "Is that all?" "Yes," I said. She put

me on hold. I waited about five minutes, then I got connected to the supervisor.

He said, "Sorry, that's not the number we need. I have never seen anything like that before." So I emailed them a picture of it. They replied, "Oh, oh, oh, well, well, that's just a 'manufacturing lot' number. The number you want is on the NAILING HEM."

There are TWO numbers??? And what the hell is a nailing hem??

Okay folks BACK IN THE CAR AND BACK TO THE CLIENT HOUSE I GO

I got out the ladder, went to the back of the house AGAIN, climbed up the ladder AGAIN, shoved the zip tool up there AGAIN, I got a hooked feel, and I pulled off the siding piece. AGAIN.

Of course, in doing it the second time, one's confidence is significantly higher. But this time I did not stop at the first number. This time I unzipped that frickin' piece of siding for over six feet.

This time, I also grabbed the siding and lifted it up until it was bent almost 90 degrees, hoping it would not crack on me, and

LO AND BEHOLD

WAY AT THE TOP – THERE WAS THE 15 DIGIT NUMBER
I wrote THAT number down, went home, and called the siding manufacturer AGAIN. They looked it up and said, "Yes, that is a siding we MADE, but sorry, we don't make it

any more."

At this point, dear reader, if you're wondering why it's so hard to get some guy to come to your house to do some simple fix for you, it's because doing the simple fixes involve these kinds of time-consuming, deflating, and frustrating experiences. They all involve time that, by the way, is seldom paid for.

Back to our story:

Then they said, "AS YOU KNOW (and no, I do not know), even if we still made it, since that siding has been out in the sun for 10 years, the color wouldn't match anyway. So why don't you go over to our local distributor with your sample and see what they can come up with? Who knows, they might have some of it in stock from years ago."

You have a local distributor?? And it's not the big box store that supposedly has everything? Sure enough, there are other "supply houses" that are fairly specialized into just a few big things like windows doors and vinyl siding. Back into the car we go.

I walked into this place which was essentially five people standing behind a counter with lots of massive three-ring binders piled up everywhere. I told them the story, and they pulled out a book of sample colors for that maker . . .

Oh, I forgot to tell you,

Every single siding manufacturer makes siding in their own unique shape, meaning that one brand of siding cannot be attached to another brand of siding. They are different dimensions and different shapes when viewed from the side, thus they will not snap together at all, even if you match the color. I started to think back to the 45 minutes spent at the big box store going through various swatch books, not being told that unless you know the maker and have the nailing hem number there is absolutely *no point* in going through the swatch books. But, I digress.

Now that I had at last found someone who kinda sorta knew what they were talking about, we started to flip through the sample/swatch book for that maker, all the while I continued to hold in my sweaty hand that that pathetic looking all dog chewed UV light bleached vinyl siding piece.

Eventually, they found something in the sample book that seemed to be a fairly close match.

But are we there yet?

Ha, ha, ha.

Not yet. The next step was, the guy at the counter went over to a computer on his desk to see if he had any of this close-as-we're-gonna-get color in stock.

After a few minutes of not very encouraging computer keyboard clicking, he turned to me and said with an extremely doubtful look on their face, "Well, it SAYS we have it in stock . . . " So, he wrote down the numbers and we went deep into the forbidden zone of the vast warehouse in the back.

Mind you, all of this was to do a fix of about two square feet. But, we strive for perfection.

We found the spot in the warehouse where they had piles of 12 foot lengths of siding. These were all odd lots, left over and returned from larger lots sold for other projects.

For all of the fancy computerized inventory software that somebody sold these guys for $150,000, in reality, we now had to grub around on the concrete floor, matching colors as best we could by eye in the dim greenish florescent light of the warehouse, all the while looking for the various teensy numbers that were stamped every six feet.

At this point, no big surprise: the closest match, the one that the computer SAID they have in stock, was nowhere to be found . . . but lying in a pile over there, there was another color, one that was kinda sorta close to it. It was not perfect, but it existed in this universe and it was in my hand.

This was one of those all too common stress laden handyman moments where a decision had to be made, even though there was no correct answer. Will the customer accept this slightly off-color piece of siding? Or should I get picky, and keep on grubbing around on this concrete floor? In the 90 degree heat? Thus risking having the warehouse guy, who, quite frankly, doesn't look all that happy or comfortable wearing a dress shirt and tie, classify me as an impossible-to-please jerk, and stop being helpful?

Close is better than nothing, so . . . I coughed up the 12 bucks or whatever is was, I walked around to the loading dock, I picked up the piece, I sawed it in half right there so it would fit in my car, and off I went. All the while, I was thinking back on how Tommy on *This Old House* had so offhandedly said "Go to the supply house and get a replacement piece."

And THAT, my friends, is HOW YOU LEARN. You just have to dig and dig and ask and look til you find instructions on how to do it and find the part or materials that you need.

As for the installation, eh . . . Just watch the vinyl siding repair video on *This Old House*. Once you have the matching replacement piece, it's EASY.

Don't Watch Me

Harking back to that garage sign that says

"Labor rates
If we do it $70 /hr
If you watch $80 /hr
If you help $100/ hr
If you worked on it before $120/ hr"

I never really understood the "if you watch" part until I started handymanning.

I suppose no one likes to have anyone "looking over their shoulder" while they work, but there is something about handymanning that is very different. Even if I like having you around, and even if I enjoy telling you all about what I am doing and how I am doing it, having another person in the room can really mess me up.

When I first experienced this problem, the best way I could define it was stage fright, sort of like the difference between singing alone in your shower vs. singing in front of someone else. But even that simile made little sense to me, since, as a former bass player, I was used to having thousands of people watch me work, and it never bothered me at all.

My best guess here is, handymanning is, in a way, very sensual work. Not in a sexual romantic way (at least not usually), but when you are screwing into a stud (pardon the phraseology), it is essential that you be fully "present" and "in the moment." Every wall stud is a unique entity; each one came from a tree, i.e., a living thing; thus, they are all just a little bit different, and you have to know just how much force to use.

If you push too hard and slip this way, you might scratch some varnish; if you overtighten a screw you might "strip" the wood, thus ruining the tenuous grip relationship between the screw threads and the hole in the stud. Then again, if it's not tightened hard enough, something may rattle or slip or stick out or fall down. And so, judging that moment when you know the screw is now tight enough and should not be turned any further is a very delicate operation, done very much by subconscious feel, requiring your full attention.

Not to belabor the point, but most handymanning tasks require intense concentration. Trying to attach a nut to a bolt that is under a cabinet, and thus out of direct visual contact, requires getting the thing on there "by feel," as you don't want to cross thread (meaning, instead of the bolt going straight in as it should, it gets going on an angle, and the threads of the bolt are now not lined up properly with the threads in the nut).

You want things to not slip, crack, or break as you apply the minimum amount of force needed to accomplish a given task. And sometimes you are daintily shaving old paint splotches off antique varnished wood, or you are chipping grout off expensive irreplaceable tiles, and of course there is the whole master chef element involved in mixing plaster and cement 'til it "feels right."

Each of these activities require a massive amount of focus, and if there is another person in the room, a person who, by the way, is usually a customer who has to be talked to in a pleasant way, it actually makes it hard to feel the materials you are working with.

You may think your handyman is being rude in ignoring you, but the fact is, to do this work well requires every available synapse be devoted to it, and nothing else. Talking to you at the same time is like texting while driving.

Moral of the story, once your handyman starts working, leave him alone.

Hidden Crud

One little item of home maintenance that no one ever seems to talk much about has to do with hidden dirt on air filters, fans, and cooling coils.

I happened upon this issue rather by chance. I was trying to help a client figure out why his electric bills were so high. As I was standing in his kitchen for over an hour doing other tasks, it eventually dawned on me that his refrigerator compressor was never shutting off.

I poked around underneath the beast to see what I could see. There was a little grate at the bottom in the front, I popped that off, and . . . oh my God.

The base of this refrigerator was one solid mass of lint. It was a grand amalgam of spider webs, dog hair, cat hair, dirt, dust, dead bugs, and God only knows what else.

At first, I was not thinking in a terribly grand strategic manner. I just knew that that amount of lint could not be a good thing. At the very least, it constituted a fire hazard, as one ember from one cigarette butt would have resulted in a grand, if perhaps short-lived, conflagration.

I got down there with a toothbrush and started to clean it out.

Well . . . much to my surprise, once I cleared away all the lint, there before me I saw . . . cooling coils. This was a surprise to me, as all the refrigerators I have ever owned had their coils in the back.

Turns out, it is very common for refrigerators to have the cooling coils installed internally at the bottom instead of in the back. By itself, that is no big deal, except . . . they tend to get covered up with all this lint. The lint acts like a down comforter, and the coils, which are there to dissipate the excess heat created in the refrigeration process, cannot function efficiently.

Once those coils are all covered up with a blanket of lint, the heat takes much longer to dissipate, thus making the refrigerator compressor work much harder to do its job. This wastes energy and causes the compressor (and the fan) to ultimately die a premature death.

One of the ongoing themes of this book is my own ignorance, and just how much stuff I have learned in the process of helping people fix odd problems with their houses. I just have to wonder why it is that I never learned about this particular item of refrigerator maintenance. On various occasions I have purchased appliances such as refrigerators and portable window air conditioners. I often see little yellow tags with dire warnings about not using extension cords and not letting babies play with the plastic wrapping. But not once . . . not once . . . have I ever seen any kind of admonishment to occasionally clean out the air filters in an air conditioner, or a dehumidifier, or the coils at the base of a refrigerator.

The added trouble with these areas of lint buildup is, they are usually accompanied by a fan that is actively blowing room air through them, thus, all the dust mite fecal matter that is in there, along with maybe all kinds of mold and bacteria, are all being blown into the house and the air you breathe therein. And we wonder why asthma is on the rise.

In another client's office condo, I came across one of those standard big whole-house heating and air conditioning systems. Depending on the season, it would blow either warm or cold air through air ducts into the various rooms. One day, as I was doing another job for them, they said, "Ya know, the air conditioning just isn't blowing very hard. What do you think?"

This could have been anything from a bad fan to a dead rat in the ducts, but I had a sneaking suspicion . . . so I went down to the big heating/cooling system they had, you know, the ones that look like a big aluminum casket. I pulled out the air filter and . . . holy moly.

The air filter, a simple, cheap, $4 item, had not been changed since Truman was president. It had gotten so blocked with dirt and hair and dust that it had literally solidified, to such a degree that no air could get through it at all. But amazingly, to the furnace manufacturer's credit, the main fan of the system so was so powerful (it was a big building) that the fan had actually been able to deform the air filter, pushing it out of the way, making it bend and contort enough so that SOME (unfiltered) air could still get through.

Think for a moment of just how much stress had been placed on this fan, shortening its life, also making it overheat. But alas, it never occurred to anyone in this building to check change the air filter.

In my limited experience, it seems that most people are far more diligent at changing their car's oil than they are doing this simple home maintenance task. For refrigerators with bottom-mounted coils, you can actually buy something called an "appliance brush" for this purpose. Keeping those air filters clean can double the life expectancy of your appliances. It saves energy, it saves money, it creates less carbon dioxide, and it keeps all that crud out of your lungs.

*   *   *

For an extra credit exercise, if you have a ventilation fan in your bathroom, you might want to take a peek at it. First, to test it, turn on the fan, then hold a square of toilet paper against the grate covering the fan. Now take your hand away. If the toilet paper square does not stay there by itself, that is, if the suction of the fan does not hold it against the grate, it may be time to do some fan maintenance.

Most of these fans are what are called "squirrel cage" fans, meaning, they are a cylinder with about 50 or more little plastic blades. They work great when new, but if these are in a bathroom, there will be a higher than usual amount of moisture in the air going through those teeny little fan blades. Over time, the dampness will make the blades collect a layer of dust-based crud. I have seen cases where these squirrel cage fans were completely blocked, and had turned into a grey cylinder that spun round and round all day while moving no air at all.

The lack of ventilation is one problem. The waste of electricity is another. I make no guarantees, and if you break it it's your problem, but to fix this issue, my method is to take a vacuum cleaner and hold a drinking straw at the end of the hose. I run the straw, which is now a flexible mini vacuum cleaner attachment, along each of the 50+ fan blades. This takes a little bit of effort, as it requires working overhead, but when you are done, as long as you didn't break the fan, you will have ventilation again. As always, to be done at your own risk!

It's Just Four Bolts

There is one element of the building trade services in general that the average person rarely thinks about. It is the presence of agents and aggregators.

One obvious example of an aggregator is the folks who run Uber or Lyft. The people who run those companies don't provide the actual service; they just act as an intermediary, hooking you up with a stranger who does the actual job of driving. They "aggregate" thousands of individual drivers into one single source.

While driving a car from point A to point B is a pretty generic, universal, just-about-anyone-with-a-car-can-do-it task, working on a house is far more complex. Handyman jobs are rarely a simple straight-ahead proposition. It's more like taking your house to the doctor.

For me the handyman, the first task is to diagnose the problem, either through seeing pictures of the problem or by seeing it in person–and reaching the diagnosis is often a massive puzzle all by itself.

Handyman Rule #2: NEVER accept anyone else's diagnosis of a problem. Always look at it yourself and make your own determination of cause and optimal fix.

Once a problem has been accurately diagnosed, to address it I then have to research the possible fixes and replacement parts needed, find them, buy them, decipher the directions if any, and then fix, refinish, paint, glue, nail, or screw the thing into place. Thus, there are far too may variables to fit the job into a nice neat little digital app.

That said, every six months or so, I get yet another call from one of these service aggregators, wanting me to work in their digital system.

I appreciate the offer, but I always turn them down, because again, in my opinion, the work is just too darn complicated. The customer's diagnosis/description of the problem is often highly unreliable, and it just generally invites disaster to ever think that something will be quick, simple, and easy.

But one day a guy called me up from one of these website driven service-providing entities, and he asked me if I would go take down an old widescreen TV, take off the existing hanging bracket hardware, move that hardware to a new TV, and then hang the new TV.

"It's just four bolts," he said.

It must've been a slow day . . . in fact, it was pouring down rain, which always makes for a slow day . . . so against my policies and procedures and better judgment, I said I would do it–as long as he paid my full hourly rate. He must've been pretty desperate to get this customer taken care of, because he agreed to it.

I was relying on the aggregator's assessment of the job, rather than doing the assessment myself. Can you hear the rumbling of low strings in a minor chord?

I drove over to the client's house. It was pouring down rain, but it was indoor work, so who cares. And sure enough, there was a broken Samsung flatscreen TV hanging on this wrought-iron tower. And remember, all I had to do was take the thing off the tower, remove the four bolts that held the mounting bracket hardware on the old TV, and attach that old bracket to the new TV, using the same four bolts. Certainly sounded simple enough. It's just four bolts.

The first thing I discovered was, the old mounting hardware on the back of this old TV was not just hanging on a hook; it was attached to this wrought-iron tower . . . with four more bolts. Suddenly, I was dealing with *eight* bolts.

As I looked at these four additional bolts, I quickly realized that they were not normal bolts. Instead, they had Allen wrench heads. (An Allen wrench head has a hexagonal hole. You need special hexagonal Allen wrenches to make them turn.)

Now, being a good versatile handyman, I do carry Allen wrenches, dozens of them. But none this big.

The only way I could get the TV off this wrought-iron tower required removing bolts five through eight. So, lacking the massive Allen wrench needed, I had to leave my entire precious toolkit in the house of a stranger, and drive to a local hardware store in the pouring rain. Suddenly this simple job . . . was not so simple.

I bought an assortment of three big Allen wrenches– I figured one of them would be right. (I was now out five dollars, but I never regret buying tools). I went back to the house, and much to my chagrin, two of them were too small . . . and one was too big. So, again, I went out into the pouring rain, drove back to the hardware store, suffered through the laughter of the clerks, and bought two more Allen wrenches, one of which would have to fit.

Once again I drove back to the customer's house, and even though the Allen head bolts were in an awkward hard-to-get-at spot, I managed to get them off. Hooray.

Thankfully, since the old TV was broken, I didn't have to treat it like anything precious. Always a bonus. I lifted the TV off the wrought iron tower, hauled it into the living room, and laid it face down on the carpet. Then I removed the original four bolts–remember them? –From the back of this old TV.

With the four bolts finally off, I removed the two old mounting brackets. Then I took the new TV out of its box (being super super careful not to drop or scratch or smudge it) and I put that face down on the carpet as well.

I took the two old mounting brackets and laid them in position over the holes in the back of the new TV. Then I took one of the four original bolts, and...

Well guess what. The bolt did not fit in the hole.

Isn't this just great. It has taken over an hour just to get the proper tools and get the old TV off the wall and the brackets disassembled, and I have run up against a wall where the parts I have are all wrong, thus I cannot proceed in a linear fashion.

Just four bolts. Yeah, right.

Now bear in mind, as a handyman, I have faced many unexpected roadblocks, ones far more difficult than the one facing me at that moment. What was so bothersome was that it was so unexpected. (Or perhaps because it WAS expected.) When I took the gig I had this lurking suspicion in the back of my mind that I would probably run into something horrible on this supposedly "easy" job. And I had.

At this point I had a choice of wussing out and leaving with tail between legs and no money, or I could handyman up and lean on this thing until it bent to my will. I chose the latter.

Being a new TV, it came with an instruction manual. I started to thumb through this thing, and sure enough, there was a spec page telling me the size of the bolts that I needed. Just to make extra sure, I actually called Samsung help (the number was right there) and they confirmed the exact size of bolt needed for the mounting hardware.

So, for the third time in two hours, I drove through the pouring rain over to the hardware store. Amazingly, they actually had this particular size of bolt.

You remember the first four bolts? Now we are up to 12 bolts. All different sizes. Allen wrenches. Jesus H.

I drove back to the customer's house AGAIN, while it was still raining cats and dogs. Again, I took the old mounting brackets and placed them over the new holes in the back of new TV. And AGAIN, I put the first bolt in the first hole. But this time, sure enough, it screwed in magnificently. I got the bolt screwed in halfway and …

It stopped.

What I had not calculated was, the bolts specified in the manual were for specific Samsung-brand mounting brackets, which, it turned out, are much thicker than the ones I had on hand.

At this point, the client happened to mention, that all their old TV mounting hardware was not Samsung brand, it all came from another brand of TV she had purchased years ago.

Okay, so AGAIN I was back in that horrific spiritually flaccid land of not having the parts to do the job. And of course I wanted to be very very careful around electronics, because the slightest little slip of an over tightened bolt and I would have a busted $500 television set. What to do?

Well, truth be told, I was thoroughly sick and tired of this whole job, so I just took a look at how far that bolt had screwed in. I took a sharpie and made little mark, and in this lady's lovely living room, I took a hacksaw and cut off an approximate amount of this bolt, spreading little metal slivers all over her Persian rug.

I filed the bolt down to get rid of any rough edges, and again, I screwed it into the hole on the back of this brand-new fancy TV, and sure enough, this time, it went all the way in.

I suppose I could have gone back to the hardware store for a fourth time and gotten a set of shorter bolts, but I just was not in the mood. Instead, I just took my hacksaw and cut the same amount off each of the remaining three bolts, and I finally managed to attach those two expletive deleted mounting brackets on the back of the new TV.

Now at this point you might think all I had to do was re-hang it on the wrought-iron tower.

But of course, you would be wrong.

You see, the locations of the holes for the two horizontal mounting brackets on the back of the new TV were vertically further apart than they were on the old TV. So on the wrought iron tower, I had to undo yet another four bolts (we are now up to 16 bolts, if you are counting) and move the lower hooks on the wrought-iron tower down to the appropriate position.

Bear in mind, even in my damp vexed state, I still had to pay very close attention and tighten these things up really well, otherwise the whole TV would come crashing down at some future date.

With the help of the resident husband, I hung the new TV on the tower, and with extreme body and hand contortions I managed to get the Allen wrench in there on the Allen Bolts to get it all properly secured.

The whole job, which was supposed to take 20 minutes, took over three hours. I was soaking wet. I got paid, but it was far more stress on me than it needed to be.

And now you know why I a) don't trust anyone else's diagnosis, b) charge by the hour, and c) don't work for aggregators.

It Smells Funny

One day a new customer called me up and said, "Every time I turn on my porch light, I get this smell of burning plastic."

Whenever you hear something like that, the entire spirit recoils in horror. You don't know what it is, so the mind spins around in all the possible worst-case scenarios that this might be.

I was not about to deal with this myself, so I called an electrician buddy and over we went. As we examined the switches and the fixtures, we discovered that somebody somewhere had run the power from the light switch out to the fixture in the porch... with speaker wire.

Not to overwhelm you with physics or anything, but electrical wire is designed to be different sizes and configurations in order to handle different amounts of electricity. Speaker wire is designed to be hooked up to amplifiers, which, on their best day, can kick out about half an amp. And this poor lady was inadvertently stressing this wire with the near maximum amount of amps it could handle before melting.

If you have ever used an electric stove element, you know what happens when electricity encounters excessive resistance: it creates heat. And we could actually see the scorch marks where the plastic was burning so hot that it was melting onto the wood and drywall.

The things you see.

Some Assembly Required

One thing that never ceases to amaze me in this line of work is the nearly universal difficulty in comprehending the directions that come with just about everything.

Now full disclosure, I have never in my life designed directions for a commercial product. However, I can't help but wonder if I couldn't do it better.

The theme of this book, again, is coping with the ignorance which is everyone's starting point in life. In this case, instead of ranting about the frustrating experience that most directions put me through, I shall try to calmly foster enlightenment. To that end, for any product-use/assembly-direction designers out there, here are my two cents:

First, if the product in question is somewhat heavy and in a bag, maybe you could put the directions somewhere other than . . . on the bag? As it is, once I pour half of a 60 lb bag of something into a hole, I now have to manhandle a 30 lb bag to find the directions and see what I need to do next. This can be vexingly inconvenient.

Next, if a powdery product like, say, tile grout, is supposed to be mixed with water, I certainly appreciate being told how much water to mix with the whole bag. But just in case I might be just doing a small patch, it would be ever so helpful to know the proper powder-to-water ratio for making smaller batches, e.g., one part powder to two parts water.

In printed directions generally, may I next suggest, using at minimum a 12 point size font? Remember, I might be reading your directions in a dimly lit basement.

Whether mixing or assembling or attaching, some steps in a given process may be far more important than others. How about making them appear as such, with a bigger or bolder font?

Another way to help the average guy would be to add some coaching. For example, if you had ten people follow the directions in a testing lab, and if more than two people make the same error, how about making a point of "When you do this next step, be careful not to make this common mistake?"

Another suggestion: how about giving some general perspective at the start for those of us who have never mixed cement before?. You know, maybe a brief paragraph at the start, something like, "If you have never mixed cement before, here is the big picture." And then tell me the usual cure times and common errors to avoid.

Now credit where credit is due: I have on occasion run into instructions for assemble-it-yourself furniture that really had their act together, especially where the included 160 assorted screws and dowels were concerned. Sometimes you do in fact get a plastic bag marked with letters, keeping all the screws well organized. Alas, this kind of experience is the exception, not the rule.

The Great Walls Not in China

As a handyman, one very common job I am asked to do is to hang things on walls, like curtain rods and pictures.

There are essentially two kinds of walls in most homes. Walls built before 1945 are usually made out of plaster. Walls built after 1945 are usually made out of drywall.

The problem is, 97% of the curtain rods and other hardware items people buy and ask me to hang on their walls are made in China. Actually, that is not the problem. The problem is, apparently, there are no plaster walls in China. The people in China who create the directions for these items are apparently completely unaware of the existence (and unique properties) of plaster walls. Thus, all of the directions that come with anything made in China will tell me how to hang things on a drywall wall, but none of them will give me any help in hanging stuff on a plaster wall.

Some definitions for you:

Drywall is an 8' by 4' by ½ inch piece of stiff material made out of gypsum. It's great stuff, which is why everyone uses it. When building a house, you just nail it to the studs, cover the seams, and you're done.

Plaster walls, however, are very different. Here is how plaster walls were made way back when:

Once the interior walls of a house were framed up (with 2x4's going floor to ceiling, spaced 16 inches apart), some guy would bring in a few hundred little pieces of wood. Each piece looked like a long yardstick.

These pieces of wood (called "lath") would be nailed onto the studs horizontally, one by one, leaving about 3/8" of space between each little piece of wood/lath.

The next day, another guy would come in, and he would spread wet plaster onto all of these little lath boards. The wet plaster would "key" into the lath, meaning, as the plaster was spread on the lath boards, it would flow through those little openings and start to fall down behind the lath boards. Thus, when it all hardened up, the plaster had a great grip on the wall of lath boards.

Again, sadly, folks in China apparently have no awareness of lath-based plaster; they think every wall in every house in the world is made of drywall. This is understandable. If no one is telling them about it, how can they know? (And yes, I must again look in the mirror, and remind myself, let he who is without ignorance cast the first bad Yelp review. Alas, my unintended theme of the common manifestation of ignorance has struck again.)

If you have an old lath plaster wall, and you try to do what the Chinese directions tell you to do– i.e., drill a big 1/4" hole and hammer in a big plastic anchor to hold your screw–when that soft plastic anchor hits a piece of wooden lath, it will just deform into a glop of bent useless plastic.
If you are dealing with plaster walls (and the lath boards that

lie within and beneath them), it is usually a much better idea to skip the anchor altogether. Instead, just drill* a tiny exploratory hole, and put a screw right through the plaster and into the lath board. For most applications, a screw in a lath board will give you plenty of grip. But if you have already blindly followed the directions, the big hole you just obediently drilled through the plaster and into the lath board (to hold a plastic anchor) is now too big to hold the regular plain screw you should have used . . . and now you are totally screwed.

PS: When you hang pictures on a lath plaster wall, don't use a nail– when the nail hits the lath board, the lath board will bend in just like a trampoline, and then push the nail right back at you. Instead (and *when drilling in to any wall, always be VERY careful not to drill into any hidden water or gas pipes or electrical lines etc.), gingerly drill a little pilot hole, and carefully screw in a 1.5 inch screw to hang your picture. Again, all to be done at your own risk!

PPS: Just because a house was built in 1920 does not mean it has plaster walls. There may have been a gut rehab in the interim, and all the walls were replaced with drywall. I have been in houses where one wall in a room was plaster, and the opposite wall was drywall. You must be constantly on your guard in this business.

YouTube Conflicts

When I first started handymanning, YouTube was a godsend. It's truly amazing just how much fabulous advice and expertise is available out there for free. In my first year of handymanning, and this is no joke, I probably watched over 3,000 home repair YouTube videos. . And to all of you folks out there who provided so much fabulous help, thank you.

That said, alas, the system is not perfect.

The problem with Youtube is, there is no filter. Pretty much anybody can put themselves up on YouTube, claiming to be an expert, telling you how to do this or that. And apparently, if you make a lot of YouTube videos, and a lot of people subscribe to and watch your videos, you can actually make money doing it. But just because someone knows how to put a video on YouTube, that does not mean they really know how to caulk a sink.

I can list several examples where people, some of whom are famous and on TV, will tell you to do a given repair procedure this way, and then a home inspector in Minnesota will tell you that that's absolutely incorrect and you should never do it that way. This can be quite vexing, as there is no third party anywhere to adjudicate the conflict.

Home repair is a world where you encounter a great deal of cognitive dissonance. It could be one person is wrong and the other is right, or perhaps they are both wrong, and here's the kicker, perhaps they are both right. Therefore you have to watch multiple videos on the same subject to at least try to make sure that the technique you are learning isn't just *a* method, but the *best* method.

Another issue that is becoming ever more prevalent: a large corporation will make a YouTube video that, by all appearances, looks like a homemade, sincere, poorly lit, poorly shot video. It will feature a guy in his basement who claims to be an independent repair guy, giving you his magic trick to doing a given process. Sad to say, in reality, he is just a soulless shill for a big company, promoting a product that is nothing special. The Russian election trolls pale in comparison.

Who's on First?

Coming back to one of the main themes of the book, there is one area where ignorance plays a major role in the life of a handyman, and that is in the environment of a hardware store.

A hardware store is a place where you acquire most of your tools and supplies for all the many jobs you do. A hardware store is also a source of information, both for what kinds of products and tools and paints to buy, but also how to do a given project. And you quickly learn that there are three levels of ignorance in your average hardware store:

The first level comes in the form of the new employees. These are often high school graduates who come to work every June. They are young, vibrant, and eager to please, but alas, since they are young, they are, by definition, inexperienced. They are still learning. They want to help, and they eagerly ask if they can help, but all too often I find they simply don't know enough to be of much assistance.

The next level comes in the form of employees who have been around for a while, but they have one tragic flaw: they cannot admit to their ignorance. This kind of person is certainly not limited to hardware store employees. I am sure you know dozens of people who think they know far more than they actually do. The problem is, in some cases these folks are unwilling to admit to any ignorance at all. If I ask, "Is this the right goop for my project?", they will never say "I am not sure" or "I don't know." Quite to the contrary, they will leap to a space of absolute certainty, and tell me that "Yes, absolutely, look no further, no question, that is what you need."

When I was just a beginner I was quick to put blind trust in the word of such people. I quickly learned (the hard way) not to do that.

Finally, and allow me to remove my hat in reverence, are the guys (mostly guys, hey, we're talking hardware) who actually know what they are talking about AND know the limits of their knowledge.

When you find a guy in a hardware store who is both knowledgeable and humble, who is eager to help but knows what he does NOT know, and will readily admit to not knowing what they do not know, those people are solid gold.

I've got a few guys at my local big box store, I have a guy at my True Value, and I even have TWO guys at my local Ace Hardware, all of whom have pulled my rear end out of the fire on numerous occasions. Without them I would be a far less effective repair person. They know how to cut glass to fit. They know where the stainless steel nails are. They can tell if a bolt is standard or metric. But again, and this is so important, they are humble, and they admit to their ignorance when they don't have a definitive answer.

It may seem counterintuitive, but the person who is quick to admit to their ignorance inspires far more confidence than the person who claims to know everything. Once you admit you don't know something, I am far more inclined to believe you when you say you DO know something else.

I often wonder just how many upper managers, especially in the big box hardware chains, understand just how much of a factor these "knowledgeable guys" are in the overall marketing scheme. I actually base my selection of the store I'm going to buy supplies from not on price, not on location, but on these guys.

If you run a hardware store and you have a really good paint guy, I will buy all my paint from you. If you've got a really good fastener and washer guy, I am going to buy all my fasteners and washers from you. Price is not an issue, because a knowledgeable guy saves me so much time, both in the store and on the job, that the slightly higher price I might pay is of no concern.

Surprise, Surprise, Surprise

Continuing with my theme of ignorance in the realm of home repair:

When I first moved into that classic old two-family house with the unvented dryer, the whole place was in near mint condition, as it had been lived in for decades by the original owners.

A few weeks after moving in, my then roommate decided to paint his bedroom ceiling. This made sense, as it was a pretty dingy white ceiling that had what appeared to be the original 1920 paint.

He went to the local hardware store, bought a gallon of high quality white latex ceiling paint, and went at it.

The first coat looked great. The next day he started to apply the second coat of paint and then, to quote Gomer Pyle:

Surprise, surprise, surprise.

All of the paint, new and old, came tumbling down in strips and sheets. Well, not all, but most.

As it turned out, many houses built in the 1920's used something called calcimine paint on their ceilings. It is essentially powdered chalk with some water and glue added. It was cheap and it looked great for a long time. BUT . . . if you get any water on it (or any water-based latex paint), it starts to dissolve. And that's exactly what happened to my roommate.

He ended up paying a guy to come over and scrape everything off so he could start all over on bare plaster. (He did not know that if he had spritzed some water on it, he could have just wiped it all off. Oh well. We do not know what we do not know.)

That was a relatively benign surprise. It gets better. Or worse.

One day a new client asked me to paint a room in her condo. I went to the hardware store and started talking to one of my guys about the project and he said to me, "You know, it's not any of my business, but it's not legal for you to paint a condo like that."

Surprise, surprise, surprise.

It turns out that here in Massachusetts, it is now illegal for an average contractor/ painter/handyman to paint a house that was built before 1978. This comes with a massive history, and some bizarre twists to the plot:

I am not a lead paint historian, but a quick summation, lead paint goes back to the Roman Empire, and all along, folks have known about the toxicity of lead paint. Even so, we have been putting lead in our paint for centuries. Lead is actually a fabulous paint additive. It holds up, it looks good, and it has great coverage. It's just horribly toxic. Hey, there's always a tradeoff.

In 1978 here in the USA we finally woke up to the idea that maybe putting a horrifically toxic brain damaging heavy metal into our homes wasn't such a great idea, and we stopped making lead paint. That still leaves us with maybe 35 million homes with lead paint still in them.

The lead in the paint on your wall right now actually isn't all that bad, if you simply leave it alone. The problem is, if you decide to RE-paint a lead-covered wall or a window, there is usually a need to do some surface scraping and sanding of the old lead paint. That can release particles of lead dust into the air.

Here in Massachusetts, if you want to paint a house that was built before 1978, you have to hire a crew of specially trained painters to do it. They hermetically seal the room, they wear hazmat suits, they keep things wet to lessen the dust, they have fancy vacuum cleaners, and they carefully dispose of all the potentially toxic old paint.

However, there is a nifty little loophole in our local laws: this rule requiring a hazmat-suit-clad painting crew only applies to painting that you, the homeowner, hire OTHER people to do. If you, the homeowner, choose to do the sanding and painting YOURSELF, there are no rules. Go wild.

This includes your disposal of the leftover lead-laced paint chips. If you are the homeowner, you can just put them out with your trash, and if five pounds of lead dust goes swirling through the neighborhood playground, well, what can I say.

Another little story: a client came to me one day and said "I have an issue with a window." I had gotten to be pretty bold with window work, so I popped over to take a look. And there . . . between the inner pane of glass and the storm window . . . was a pile of grey pebbles. It looked like one of those ant farms that kids play with.

There was a momentary "what the hell is this?", but then I looked closer and realized that this window was half filled with . . . Vermiculite.

Vermiculite is a kind of light porous rock that was once used as attic insulation material. You would take a 30 pound bag of these pebbles and just pour it out in your ceiling between the joists. In fact, the reason I recognized it so quickly was because way back when, in the very same apartment that I shared with my cascading paint roommate, I had done just that; I had dumped hundreds of pounds of this stuff all through my attic.

Back to the ant farm window, it dawned on me that the attic of this house had probably been filled with vermiculite as well, and the vermiculite had, like sand in an hourglass, found a hole somewhere and had poured down into this window.

I just love solving nifty unusual problems like this, and I added this window cleanup to the list of many things this house needed. The next day, I happened to mention this bizarre issue to someone in the trades. He looked at me and said . . . "Uh . . . you do know that stuff is full of asbestos, right?"

SURPRISE, SURPRISE, SURPRISE

NO I did NOT know it had asbestos in it. I went running to Google and sure enough, turns out this stuff was mined in

Montana somewhere. For decades, thousands of tons of vermiculite had been bagged up and sold all over everywhere. But then someone realized there was a deposit of asbestos near the mine. OOPS. Now, while not every bag of vermiculite they shipped had asbestos in it, we have to assume that they all do, because we don't know which bag came from what mine, it's so hard to test for it, and the stuff is so very very toxic.

Suddenly, what started as a simple hole plugging-task had turned into a mini superfund site. Yeesh.

All I could do for this lady was advise her to pull the shade.

Just fyi, the rule of thumb about this kind of toxic stuff is to simply leave it where it is and don't disturb it. But in her case, it is still trickling down into the window . . .

Another story: one day a customer called me and asked me to help clean up a cement floor, to prep for her new carpeting. The old carpet and pad had already been removed. The floor was now bare cement, but at some point this cement floor had been covered with linoleum tiles, and it still had a lot of black gunk all over, which was likely the adhesive for the old tiles. We decided we would try to clean it up.

I went looking for some magic chemical that might serve to help clean up this layer of black goo, and as I asked someone at a hardware store about what they had to offer, they looked at me and said . . "Uh . . .you do know that stuff may contain asbestos, right?"

SURPRISE, SURPRISE, SURPRISE

Turns out that "black mastic," i.e., a black adhesive used for flooring in American homes for many decades, was often made with asbestos as an added ingredient. Yikes. I had no idea.

I have since discovered that Asbestos can be found in all kinds of unexpected places in older homes. Popcorn textured ceilings, insulation, various adhesives, and some kinds of old roofing shingles can all have asbestos buried within.

Again, our theme of ignorance has reappeared. I am not particularly thrilled about announcing to the world how terribly ignorant I am about some things, but I thought this was good information for you, dear reader, to know, thus it is worth the embarrassment.

I will say though, that while I am amazed at just how much of this horrifically toxic stuff there is out there, I am even more amazed at how seldom we are warned about it. Yes, when you buy things at a paint store, they will post warnings about lead paint, but there are precious few public service announcements about the common occurrences of asbestos in your house. You could very well be walking on it or under it right now. Again, the bugaboo of ignorance. The possible presence of this very dangerous stuff in your home should be common knowledge, but it isn't.

Psychic Income

While I do spend a fair amount of time complaining about the challenges of handyman work, to be fair, there is a major plus side to it that bears mentioning. It is the straight-out sense of accomplishment, and job satisfaction.

For example, sanding a floor is hard work, and I don't do it very often. But there is something wonderful in manhandling a big drum sander, slowly removing 80 years' worth of ground-in dirt, wax, and spilled coffee to reveal the long lost gorgeous old white oak beneath. Such work creates a visceral sense of making the world a better place, in a very tangible way.

I have never actually gone out of my way to drive past a house I have fixed, but when my route does take me past one, I love to turn my head and see that the mailbox I installed last year is still there, functioning and looking fabulous.

Another bonus to handyman work is, I often find myself living in eternal kindergarten. Hardware stores sell lots of nifty toys (we call them tools of course), and playing with them is just plain fun. I also get to make things, paint things, glue things, bust things up, and get delightfully dirty too. The only thing missing is the glitter.

There is also a very satisfying aesthetic/artistic element of the work. Caulking a bathtub may sound like a rather pedestrian task, and yes, it can be done in a quick minimalistic way to achieve functionality and no more. But if you choose, you can literally transform a bathtub or any other space in a home, taking it from nothing special to palace, just by taking a little care to make the little elements look right. It takes time of course, along with a fair amount of skill. You can make a huge improvement in a room just by putting a new coat of pain on the walls. But on those same walls, if you first fix all the tiny little pits, cracks, lumps, or other blemishes, and THEN paint it, the difference can be astounding. And that difference is felt every time anyone walks into that room.

Whenever I see a bit of sloppy work or an unfixed blemish, I refer to it as "insult to the spirit." It's a subtle thing, and we usually just learn to live with it. Still, such things can feel like a crime, or at the very least, an act of oppression. Thus the handyman becomes crime fighter hero, protecting the soul from subtle aesthetic evil. It's never perfect, but making things look right or hang straight, and doing the work in such way that it will look good, not just this week, for many years after, is immensely rewarding. It also has a huge impact on the customer's quality of life, just as much as any painting they may hang on the wall you just fixed.

Schrödinger's Shower

About once a month I will be doing a basic handyman job for a client, and at the end of the day they will say "Would you mind taking a quick look at something?" All too often, they will proceed to show me evidence of a water leak that has stained or even destroyed a wall or a ceiling.

With few exceptions, the problem is never caused by an original 50-year-old shower stall or tub enclosure. Instead, it's always a tub or shower that was remodeled 3-5 years ago.

After repeatedly running into variations of this same issue, I decided to educate myself on the topic of tub enclosures and shower stalls. I have no intention of ever building one of these, but I wanted to know enough to at least offer decent advice to my clients. Alas, when I started to do my research, I encountered a morass of contradictory information– far more than what exists on any other topic of home maintenance. The only way I could make sense of it is by use of quantum mechanics.

Those of you who are students of physics, or at least fans of the television show "Big Bang Theory," may be familiar with the concept of Schrödinger's cat.

Hopefully not to bore you too much, there is this idea in quantum mechanics that says tiny little particles of matter can exist in two different states at the same time. They only stop doing this, and snap into one state or the other, when they are observed by someone.

To illustrate this idea, a physicist named Schrödinger invented a virtual cat in a box. The box also contained a vial of poison that would open at some random time. Prior to opening the box and observing the cat, we can think of the cat as being in two different states at the same time, i.e., both alive and dead. (PETA folks, please do not send me any nasty letters, it's not a real cat, and besides, this was all Schrödinger's idea, not mine.) Only when we open the box and observe the cat does the cat flip to one state or the other.

As strange as that may sound, and with all due respect to physicists around the world, quantum mechanics are fairly simple compared to shower stalls and tub enclosures.

The reason I say that is, once you observe a particle that was previously in two different states, it makes up its mind, and it becomes one or the other. Shower stalls do not do this.

Instead, I have come to accept the bizarre fact that tub enclosures and shower stalls exist in two completely different opposite states all the time. And, unlike the relative simplicity of quantum mechanics, where the act of observing something makes it resolve into one state or the other, even if you observe a shower stall all day, and maybe even bring your friends over to have a look, it will remain in what physicists call a "superposition" of being both this and that at the same time. This can be quite vexing.

Just to quickly list some of the superpositions of shower stalls and tub enclosures:

–You must never use drywall to build the walls of a shower
      enclosure. Instead, you must use special wall
      material like cement board.
–It is perfectly fine to use drywall to build the walls of a
shower
      enclosure.

–You should never use grout to seal the corners of shower
stall
–It is perfectly fine to use grout to seal the corners of a shower
      stall

–Water always travels downhill.
–Water sometimes travels uphill (this is known as "capillary
      action")

–A shower stall must be completely waterproofed with
      a sealant before installing the tile.
–You don't need to use a sealant.

–In a "shower pan," a sloped layer of mortar must be installed
      underneath the rubber liner.
–It is totally unnecessary to place a sloped layer of mortar
      underneath the rubber liner.

–Grout is waterproof.
–Grout is not waterproof.

–Always use grout sealer.
–Never use grout sealer.

–An eighth inch gap between tiles should be filled with
      unsanded grout.

–An eighth inch gap between tiles should be filled with sanded grout.

Sigh. At least you can count on the cat to make a decision.

Whenever I do research on doing a kind of job that I've never done before, a consensus eventually emerges regarding the best way to do most jobs. Unfortunately, when it comes to shower stalls, there is no such consensus. Granted, there are many people who all claim to know the answer, but it's a little bit like different master chefs telling you how to make beef bourguignonne.

There may be some monk on a mountaintop in the Himalayas who has figured it all out, but he's not talking. The people who ARE willing to talk about building shower stalls, either via books, YouTube videos, online articles, or just casual conversation, simply do not agree. There is no clear master authority. Everybody has their way of doing it, and for most of them, their way to do it is the only way to do it.

I confess, I do find it odd that for all the research being done in universities on so many arcane aspects of life, to my knowledge, no one has ever researched the optimal way to build a shower stall.

*   *   *

I once had a client who had done a recent bathroom remodel, and she had yet another of these oh-so-common less-than-perfect tub enclosures.

On the day the work was finished, it was absolutely gorgeous; but within a day or two, she couldn't help but notice a horrific smell of sewage.

Fortunately, this occurred just a few days after the installation, so the installers were still in business and answering her calls. They came back, and after a cursory examination, it was collectively realized that this tub had no P trap.

If you don't know what a P trap is, well, Plumbing 101: every drain in your house works very much like your toilet, in that, the drain pipe goes down, and then it comes back up again to create a U-shape. A certain amount of water always lives in that "U"– you can see half of it when you look into any basic toilet. It is essential to have that water standing in your toilet, because that bit of water is all that stands between you and all the pungent gases that live in your local town sewer system. Ick. (Please don't ask me why they don't call it U trap instead of a P trap. I honestly don't know. Not sure I want to.)

The tub installer guys came back, and since they had not put the pipes in properly at the start when they had everything open and before they had put the tub in place, they had to punch a hole in the ceiling downstairs to get access to the problem area, and install the P-trap.

This same tub with the missing P trap had another problem, which was, the tub itself was not sloped properly. "Sloped" is VERY big deal when installing anything in a bathroom, as an

100

incorrect slope means water will go down that incorrect slope into a place you don't want it to go.

This tub was not level. Instead, it was sloped outward just a half of a degree, and that was just enough to make drops of water that were supposed to trickle back into the tub (and down the drain) go out into the front of the tub and over to the drywall wall.

Again, had this been done with cement board etc., even with the improper slope this would not have been much of a problem but . . . there it was.

I do wish to emphasize, there are thousands, perhaps tens of thousands, of skilled craftsmen who go about the country all day every day installing shower and tub enclosures who know what they are doing. That said, on average, at least once a month, someone will show me a defective shower/tub installation, with either tiles coming loose or some kind of water leak. (That does not include the common issue of mold in cracked grout). This sort of problem is somewhat insidious, because a water-related error may not become obvious for a few years after an installation. When it finally does appear, the fix can be a pretty severe rip out and replace.

Again, this is just part of my overall theme of witnessing ignorance morphing into destructiveness. We all live in the shadow of the monster of ignorance. It is lurking constantly, and you never know when or how it will strike. Forewarned is at least somewhat forearmed.

*   *   *

I have to tell you, as a handyman I fear water more than any other element in a house. Granted, gas and electricity are dangerous, but at least they have the decency to kill you quickly and get it over with. Water, on the other hand, is slow-moving liquid fire. Water causes mold. Water causes stains. Water attracts centipedes, ants, termites and other vermin. Then it destroys drywall, then it destroys framing.

Water is just so very sneaky. It leaks out of water pipes, but it also leaks in through the roof, sometimes a yard sprinkler shoots it through a window, and sometimes it just condenses out of thin air. Some small electrical "leaks" can be prevented with an arc fault breaker. Small gas leaks will just waft away. But if water is seeping in somewhere, even in tiny amounts, it is a malevolent entity that will silently and relentlessly seek to destroy your house, drop by drop, inch by inch.

*　*　*

One day a friend of mine was looking at a new apartment and she asked me to come along for moral support. When we showed up, it was quite a party: the landlord/owner was there, the rental agent was there, and there were at least two other potential renters in attendance as well.

It was an old 1920's house that was in pretty good shape, a little funky here and there, but it had character.

I left the main tour group and walked into the master bath. The original tub enclosure had been fitted over with one of those form-fitting acrylic covers. They are not as nice as tile, but it's an economical way to upgrade.

This tub enclosure was unusual in that there was an original wooden window above the tub, and the acrylic enclosure had been custom made to allow for this window.

The window caught my eye for some reason. Perhaps I was curious to see if the sash cords were still in place, so I decided to get a closer look. To do this I had to step into the tub itself. As I did so . . .

Squish.

When my foot hit the bottom of the tub, I could feel that there was a layer of water under it, lying between the new acrylic shell and the old tub underneath.

These acrylic covers are supposed to be form fitted and caulked to death, but, obviously . . . something was a tad askew. It was yet another bad installation.

The cavalcade of interested parties on the grand tour gradually drifted into this bathroom. I had the awkward duty to inform the realtor, the owner, and the several previously somewhat interested but now not at all interested potential renters about this odd little situation. This was an issue that would involve sizable costs as well as a general disruption of the living space, as these custom made enclosures take a while to create and ship, plus all the removal of the old and installation of the new once it arrived.

I guess you had to be there, but it was kind of awkward, tragic, and funny all at the same time.

The things you see.

A Cement Bullet

One day a new client called with a typical list of household fixes, but then she added something new: her mailbox was mounted on a post out by the road, the whole assembly had fallen over, and she wanted it fixed.

The fix, in this case, was to mount the mailbox post in cement.

I do not like cement.

It's nothing personal, I have never been offended or mistreated by cement. It's just that, as a handyman, you can't really ever get super specialized, as you do so many different tasks, and cement is just very unforgiving. You're essentially mixing sand into a bunch of very strong glue. Once you add the water, the clock starts running, with no do-overs. It's heavy, it's hard, it's rough, and while it doesn't seem to be very sticky when it's wet, once it dries, it will fossilize itself onto anything nearby. And if it sticks to something you didn't want it to stick to, good luck chiseling it off later.

In such situations, Murphy's Law ("Anything that can go wrong, will go wrong") weighs heavily upon the mind.

But this job seemed doable. There was no need to mix the

105

cement beforehand. The idea was to dig a little hole, pour a 60 lb bag of unmixed/dry quick setting cement in said hole, mount the post in the dry powder, put in some water, let it harden for 20 minutes, and you're all done.

When you are working with chemicals that "cure," that is, chemicals that harden in a fairly short time via chemical reactions, well, it's nice that they harden up so fast, but its also quite nerve racking. This anxiety is made ever so much worse when you are dealing with an unfamiliar compound. You find yourself reading the directions over and over again, making sure you are following every single step to the letter. One single screw-up and you will have a 60 pound mistake on your hands– one that you will have to dig up, lift up, haul away, and dispose of on your own time.

I dug the hole, the whole time wondering if I should call 1-800-DIGSAFE, but I figured, my little eight dollar shovel is not likely to cause much harm going a foot down. I managed to dig the hole without incident. Then, the genie was about to be let out of the 60 lb. bottle. I poured the powdery stuff into the hole, and then I worked the post down into it.

And now, the moment of truth, the point of no return: the directions said to pour a gallon of water into the powder in the hole, at which point, so said the bag, I would have about 20 minutes to mess about with leveling the post. Great.

Since the post was already mounted in the dry powder, I said to myself, "Oh what the hell, as long as we're here, let's get this thing leveled so it will be close to all set when the water goes in."

I checked the post for level and it seemed fine. At this point, I was mostly wondering what I would do for 20 minutes after I poured the water, as I would have to hold the post in level place until the cement "set up," that is, until it fully hardened.

I poured in the water and . . . much to my surprise, the cement fully hardened . . . in about 4 seconds. Hard as a rock. WHOA.

Didn't expect THAT. Where's my wiggle room window of 20 minutes before setup???

As it turned out, since it was a murderously hot and humid day, that ambient heat and moisture affected the chemicals. The setup time had been reduced from 20 minutes to less than five seconds. Without notice.

Note, the day before, I had actually called the concrete manufacturer's support line to talk things through, and they did not mention any of this as a possibility. Even with all that humble and overt effort to de-ignorance myself, I still had a gremlin leap out at me.

It was pure luck (or perhaps the handyman gods taking pity on me) that I had altered the order of the process, and I had leveled the post before I poured in the water. Had I not done that leveling first,, it would have been a total disaster. As it was, I was saved the 20 minute wait. Yay.

If you are not expecting a bullet to come your way, and one whizzes by your head out of the blue, it takes a moment to fully realize what just happened. But when you do realize what just happened, you get quite a flush of fear and anxiety and relief all at once. I had dodged a cement bullet that I was not expecting.

Some days you just get lucky.

The Smoke Detector Always Chirps Twice

Early in my handyman career, a nice but rather frantic young lady called me up to ask for help with a beeping smoke detector.

The incessant beeping was annoying enough, but she had an added wrinkle: she had to leave the house for work and leave her dog at home. This smoke detector of hers was doing a full volume dead battery chirp every 2 minutes, and it was driving her dog absolutely insane. The dog was chewing up the doors and the carpet and the chairs or whatever.

This particular smoke detector was a truly ancient model. She emailed a picture. It looked like the insides of a Macintosh computer had been nailed to her ceiling. The normal procedures of disabling a smoke detector did not apply to her situation.

At the time, I lacked the knowledge necessary to fix her problem, but it was such a vicariously traumatic experience I never forgot it. Ever since that day I have paid close attention whenever anyone talks about chirping smoke detectors.

There are many things in the realm of home construction that are very nonintuitive. For example, when I go to a lumber yard, I have come to accept the fact that when they sell me a 2x4, it isn't really a 2x4, it's a 1-1/2 by 3-1/2. I also have come to accept that while 14 is generally thought to be a larger number than 12, 14 gauge electrical wire is actually *smaller* than 12 gauge electrical wire.

But smoke detectors . . . smoke detectors offer up a whole 'nother level of confusion, at least for me.

I am often hired to install smoke detectors. I don't do the hard wiring, but I put in hard-wired replacements and new battery-operated ones all the time. Whenever I am hanging something in someone's house, I always try to be mindful of the feng shui, and install the thing so it looks nice and level and balanced. But whoever makes smoke detectors is not very helpful in this department. There is no marking on the mounting plate to tell me where top dead center is, and since the detector twists onto the mounting plate, and they are all different designs, I have to make my best guess as to what will result in a nice 90 or 180 degree angle. The only way to do it truly right is by trial and error. That means I would have to turn the ceiling into a Swiss cheese as I drill and re drill. Better to compromise and just leave it.

Maybe everyone else in the world already knew this, but I sure didn't: there are two different kinds of smoke detectors. One is "ionization," the other is "photo electric." And again, bear in mind, I am a neophyte here, but apparently the former is designed to detect smoke from a hot flaming fire, and the latter is better at detecting smoke from a smoldering low level fire. So I guess you have to think about what kind of smoke you would prefer to be alarmed about. You *can* buy smoke detectors that are sensitive to both kinds of smoke, but they are not standard.

The next thing I truly do not understand is how smoke detectors are so often designed to actually invite disablement. Many detectors have a light that flashes every 30 seconds or so. Let's see . . . people trying to sleep . . . flashing light . . . what is wrong with this picture? Pardon me for uttering the obvious blasphemy: this flashing light is an incentive to remove the alarm, and hide it in a drawer or the trunk of your car.

Next, there is the issue of nuisance alarms, i.e., a smoke alarm going off because of cooking bacon and eggs with too much gusto. That by itself encourages disablement, but on top of that, there is the "cry wolf" factor. Question: when you hear a smoke detector going off, do you immediately grab your baby pictures and passport and run into the street in your underwear? Or do you assume that it's just a false alarm, and ignore it? If people are being conditioned to ignore an alarm, that is similar to disabling it.

And finally, one thing I simply cannot understand is the design of the dead battery chirp.

We live in an age of extraordinary technical innovation, but smoke detectors are not keeping up with the rest of the class. It is amazing how often people will call me to fix a smoke detector that started to chirp at 3 am.

There is actually a reason why this 3 a.m. chirp experience happens so often: it's because batteries become less efficient when they get cold. 3 a.m. is when your house gets the coldest. So if a smoke detector's battery is near death, it will choose to sound its death knell when the house is coldest, which means it will start that sleep-killing once a minute chirp at 3 a.m. I could understand first-generation 1985 era smoke detectors having such primitive functionality and being so very user unfriendly, but I think it odd that nothing has changed. I fixed two of these just last week. (Note, there are some new detectors coming out that are sensitive to daylight/darkness cycles in order to ameliorate this problem. Let's all celebrate that someone noticed the problem, but as of the date of this writing, this feature is not standard issue.)

Also, if you have two or three alarms mounted in close proximity, the acoustic properties of the chirp noise are such that it can be very hard to tell which alarm is doing the chirping. Since there is no sure way to tell which one needs a new battery, the quickest way to get back to sleep is to disable ALL of the smoke detectors.

Smoke detectors will not work at all if they are disabled, and if you design them in such a way that you force the owner to disable them in order to get a decent night's sleep, this is, to me, pretty nonsensical. Just my opinion.

P.S. Finally, a little inside trick: when you start to replace interconnected hardwired smoke detectors, (and you should do this every ten years at least) it is a good idea to replace them all with the same brand. Sure, if you don't, they should still all talk to eachother without an issue, but if you mix and match, well . . . good luck.

Handyman Hatha Yoga

One of the grand misconceptions about being a handyman, or, for that matter, being a welder, plasterer, electrician, or plumber, is that in these jobs you "work with your hands."

While this is more or less correct, you work, not just with your hands, but with your entire body, including your brain. It's a much more holistic way of being, as you use your whole body, mind, and spirit in your work.

It is very common to simply leap to the cultural contention that any work involving coordination of your biceps and your quadriceps, and the use of them at their highest levels of potential force, is somehow a lower level of being. I challenge this concept.

If anything, the work is a higher level of being, as you not only have to do the abstract "knowledge work" to understand the problem at hand, you must also design a process for executing a solution, and then you must also execute that process with the fingers, arms, and tools you have on hand.

It's easy to feel superior to those who struggle directly with a given physical task, because in the abstract, the problem always looks so simple. But in the field, there is always some unknown gremlin or obstacle that no one thought of back at the office. Usually it has to do with a pipe or a load bearing beam that cannot be moved. It must be got round to get at the original thing that, if it was up on top, any idiot could unscrew and replace. It's the unexpected obstacle that requires so much added brainwork as well as muscle work.

Just one example:

A customer called and said she had a leaky hose bib on her house. In case you don't know what that is, most houses have a spigot, called a hose bib, on the outside of the house, usually located about 3 feet off the ground. This is where you hook up a hose so you can water your grass or whatever.

Leaky faucets don't seem like much of a problem, especially when they are outside, but if you were to put a bucket under a leaky hose bib, you would soon learn that even though it's a single drip every second or so, over the course of the day you have just paid for 15 gallons of water. Such problems need to be fixed.

If you look on YouTube, you will find several suave confident well dressed experts who will take you through the process of fixing a leaky hose bib. The first step (after you turn off the water) is to "simply" unscrew the locking nut.

Simply. I just love it when someone says "simply" about anything. The chances of it being simple, I have learned, are less than .02%. If it was simple you would not need to make a YouTube video about how to do it. Nor would anyone call me to come do it for them.

That said, according these calm confident YouTube presenters, once you "simply" unscrew the hose bib, you "simply" replace a little washer inside, screw it all back on, and you're done. It looks like a job that will take all of 10 minutes. Don't they all.

If you are making a delightfully well-lit video with a brand new right-off-the-shelf brand new hose bib, OF COURSE it will come right off. But in the real world, hose bibs have been out in the rain and snow for 40 years. Variables are thus introduced, and they are never helpful.

Anyway, having watched this nonchalant hose bib fix Youtube video, I casually set about to SIMPLY unscrew this hose bib. I put a nice big pipe wrench on it, put a little force on it, and…

Nothing. No movement. My existence was disregarded.

Hmmm . . . suddenly, things are not so simple.

Realizing I had to put considerably more force on it than originally planned, I put some vice grips on the part of the pipe coming out the house (because I knew that the amount of force I was about to exert could conceivably twist the soft copper pipe upstream of the hose bib).

I braced my feet hard on the ground, got a good angle, and I pushed hard towards the right of the hose bib base while I pushed hard left with the pipe wrench. I was also very careful not to risk catching my hands in a scissors motion of the two wrench handles if they were to let go and suddenly meet.

Nothing. This supposedly simple thing . . . simply would not move.

I took a moment to mutter a quiet curse towards that guy on

YouTube who had said "you SIMPLY unscrew the hose bib..."

Simply? This is not simply.

Obviously, this hose bib nut had rusted somewhat, and so for all intents and purposes, it was virtually welded on.

This was one of those *High Noon* handyman moments, when heartless adversity is staring you in the face . . . and you and you alone must face it, as the only other option is to give up and go home with a pocketful of shame and no money.

What to do?

There's always the option of just quitting, and admitting that this brainless soulless inert piece of metal has defeated you. But that just rankles to the core of one's handy manliness. It is now you, lone handyman, against the universe. You're also working against the last person who worked on this, who perhaps tightened this thing down as hard as they could to lessen an original leak. Then there are the chemical processes of corrosion and oxidation, all conspiring against you to prevent you from achieving your goal. And to top it all off, as an added bonus, the situation brings back vivid memories of all the times in your life when anyone told you that you could not have what you wanted. It's like a therapy session on steroids.

Again, while there is the immediate interaction with physical reality in this work, all of it is really just an extension of work of the mind. Much of it is about solving problems. Many times these are unique problems where no one else has ever come up with a fix, because this is the first time this problem has occurred.

So . . . the thing won't move. You start to think about ways to MAKE it move.

There is always the option to accept the difficulty of a given job like this, meaning, there is always the option to just give up. But in handymanning, when the physical world does not bend to your will, you get a little crazy. It creates a kind of Captain Ahab obsession . . . and this stinking little rusted hose bib had become my white whale du jour. I was going to get that thing off of there, or die in the attempt.

Sometimes you start talking to yourself. This hose bib was saying to me, "You can't have the money you thought you were going to get today because I, hose bib, will not let you."

"Really? Well, Mr. Hose Bib, all I can say is,

"F**k you. I will not leave here until you bend to my will."

(Note, when you start talking like this to hose bibs that are standing in the way of your ultimate goal, it is a gateway drug to talking in the exact same manner to human beings who might also be standing in the way of your ultimate goal.)

I drove to the hardware store and got a big bottle of penetrating oil. (Penetrating oil is designed to soak into these kinds of bolts and nuts, and soften the rust that has made them freeze up and stick so hard.)

I sprayed on the penetrating oil, with high hopes that it would soak in and free up the rusted metal threads. I waited for about 15 minutes, then I went back at it with the full force of my toughest wrenches.

[Insert sound effect here of groan caused by massive tension on major muscle groups]

And, nothing.

This was getting serious. At this point it's as if some primal kill-or-be-killed instinct had welled up within me, It was no longer about the money or the customer. It was a gauntlet thrown down at the core of my manhood. An element of animal savagery took hold. At such moments of handyman passion it is difficult to remain rational and ask the question, "Is this really worth it?" You just get crazy.

I sprayed on some more penetrating oil and decided to let the oil do the work overnight. I came back the next day, I sprayed on some more penetrating oil, waited 5 minutes, and gave it another massive attempt of the absolute nth degree of my physical capability.

And that expletive deleted-ing thing simply would not move.

Okay, now things have entered into the realm of simply you against the physical universe, and you're either going to win big or you're going to lose big. And I had no intention of losing, big or otherwise.

But I also knew that my mere physical self, by itself, had been defeated, so I had to transcend the mere physical aspect and employ some higher level brain activity.

Grasping at straws for any outside help I could get, I took some aluminum foil and essentially created a little bowl around this stuck hose bib nut, and I poured about a cup of this penetrating oil into it, immersing the nut. I then left it to soak in overnight.

117

The next day I came back, and at this point, I had decided it's this thing or me, and I was not going take no for an answer.

Again, I put the vice grips around the base of the hose bib pipe, and I put the wrench on the other side of the nut, getting the best angle that I could do that would allow maximum use of my physical strength.

Perhaps you've read of those stories of people on some drug like PCP, where they acquire momentary superhuman physical strength and can lift a car. This was one of those moments. I brought myself to a super high level of physical force, and sure enough,

That nut came loose.

A couple of pieces of metal moving about an inch may not sound like very exciting stuff. But in that brief moment, I felt like I was king of the world. I had defeated mine enemy. I was a hero.

When you spend each day overcoming the physical resistance of rust-frozen pipes, or moving 125 pound planters across the lawn, or pulling 4 inch nails out of walls, a sense of confidence and power gradually manifests within. When you constantly bang up against the challenges of modifying the physical world, you find yourself repeatedly sharpening your manhood on a whetstone of harsh physical adversity. The end result, quite frankly, is delicious.

There is a feeling of victory that comes with this kind of work, when you prevail over the physical universe. You have made the physical world bend to your will even though it had resisted you with enormous power. This kind of experience changes you. It bestows a kind of hard confidence on you that no amount of success at knowledge work can ever provide.

*   *   *

The purely physical challenges of handyman work, especially when I first began, were quite daunting. In my first job, I was hired to mostly build shelves. This did not require extreme feats of strength. It was more just ongoing physical actions of lifting lumber, inserting about 85 screws, and then moving the moderately heavy completed shelves a few yards. But whether you're lifting a few boards or just holding a drill, it's more the fact that you're not sitting in a chair or standing upright. Instead, you are constantly holding yourself in odd positions. I call this "handyman yoga."

For example, some days might involve scraping old paint off a water damaged ceiling. This might require holding one's arms overhead for 30 minutes, or maybe two hours, straight. Assembling bunk beds from Wayfair or IKEA requires spending four to six hours on your hands and knees, as you often have to use the floor as a work surface. It's not the work itself that is so hard, it's the odd body positioning required to do it. If you're not used to this kind of work, believe me, you'll feel it the next day.

In my first few months of doing handyman work, I often felt like a gas stove whose pilot light had gone out. I had never been so tired in my entire life. There were many days where I wondered if I was going to be able to keep it up. Sometimes I felt so worn out, just asking my legs to climb a flight of stairs seemed like a rather extreme request, as all the little fibers in my muscle tissue had used up all of their calcium grip and just wanted to call in sick.

But the human body, at virtually any age, is an exceptionally adaptable instrument. After six months of handyman yoga, my body simply adjusted. I now exist in a physical body that has developed an astonishing level of strength. Carrying a 40 pound toolkit around does amazing things to your physique. And on top of that, there is an added bonus, of what can only be called "toughness."

I used to wonder how football players could go out and play in five degree weather with no sleeves. Now I understand. If you expose your body to physical adversity on a regular basis, after a while, it simply learns to disregard cold, fatigue, and pain. That cold, fatigue, and pain are still there, but your mind no longer perceives them. You can cut your hand and be bleeding profusely, but you just shrug it off. The blood will clot eventually, the skin will heal up in a week or two, but for now, we got work to do.

Perfect Scores

One of the most difficult culture shocks I encountered upon entering into the world of handymanning was the degree of imperfection that was simply inherent in the work.

When I was in school, I was a pretty good student. I often received "perfect scores" on tests I took. And when I worked as a professional musician, while the occasional wrong note was tolerated, for the most part, the whole idea, and the ideal standard of performance, was to be "mistake free."

I must confess, part of why I so much enjoyed doing work at the "no mistake" level was, it protected me from any stray criticism. Alas, handymanning does not give me any such protection. The whole concept of achieving "perfect scores" simply does not apply to this kind of work. At least, not very often.

If you were to look through the 3/8 inch thick layer of drywall that is our usual immediate visual environment, you would see a world that is nailed and stapled together in a very inexact, dangling participle, sentence fragment, double negative, its when you meant to say it's, C-minus kind of way.

There are shims making drawers just barely work; there are

knob-and-tube circuits in the walls with no ground wire, and maybe no insulation; there are smoke detectors that are over 20 years old. Sometimes the house has settled and nothing is plumb.

As a student, my goal was to get a perfect score on every test, and I often succeeded. Now, in facing the many dimensions of home repair, in addressing the necessity for shelter and making the doors and windows and locks just minimally work, I have come to accept D- as the standard for success. Of course, I try to do every job as best I can, but most of the time, I am simply trying to restore minimal functionality. It's often a binary situation: an 80-year-old doorknob either works or it doesn't. In such cases, anything above an F is fabulous.

This brave new "real" world, consisting of stone, tile, cement, plaster, wood, hardware, and screws that were all originally assembled 80 years ago, is a universe of endless compromise. There is only so much time, there is only so much money, there is only so much hardware directly applicable to your intention, and the level of execution that a customer is willing to pay for varies on a daily basis. There is no possibility of getting an A+, because no matter how well I wire up a lamp, the wire has some resistance, thus even on its best day it still generates waste heat. It is a passing grade, it is adequate, but it is not perfect, ever. And because it is not perfect, I feel endlessly vulnerable. But amazingly, my clients are consistently thrilled if the thing works at all. No one ever asks for perfection, and they even tell me to stop when I try to achieve it.

Horrible to Close Enough

Before becoming a handyman, I spent a fair amount of time poking around in the rarified world of management theory. There are a great many books on the topic, with more published every day.

But there is one problem with all of these books, which is, they all seem to be aimed at corporate success. There seem to be precious few success books directed at a guy driving around in a pickup truck fixing dangling downspouts and broken windows.

So, for those sole proprietors who may feel that they have been glossed over in this massive miasma of management methodology, here are some of my favorite handyman business management success techniques. It's certainly not *Good to Great* but they have helped to take me from *Horrible to Close Enough*:

Technique #1: The "Three Strikes" Rule

Most corporate management advice is about constantly
increasing sales and acquiring more and more customers, but
when you work alone and offer a service that people are
already clamoring for, you have an opposite problem, which
is, how to filter out unwanted time-and-energy-wasting
problem clients.

While the vast majority of new customers who call out of the
blue are delightful people, in any human endeavor there is
always the possibility of running into someone who is a source
of negative energy. Real problem clients are actually pretty
rare, but every tradesperson still has to learn how to recognize,
handle, and preferably avoid them.

The "three strikes rule" is a customer-filtering technique I
learned from a locksmith. I use this method all the time. Here
is an example of how it works:

A new customer calls and asks for some service to be done.
Along with the usual inquiries as to what needs to be done, I
ask about certain things that might tell me that this is a less-
than-appealing job that should be turned down. No job is
perfect, but this rule helps you know when the line has been
crossed. For example:

If they are located outside my normal 10 mile service radius,

Strike one

If the job they need done is outside my skill range, or is just a really aggravating kind of job like anything on a floor or a ceiling, or there is a better than 50-50 possibility that I will get wet whilst doing it:

Strike two

And, most especially,

If they have an attitude problem, . . .

STEEEEEE–RIKE THUH– REEEEEEE

Of course, an annoying attitude can get them three strikes all by itself, but you get the idea. Difficulty in parking in an overbuilt gentrified neighborhood, a need for the use of noxious chemicals, working outdoors from November to March . . . all of these can get a strike. It is a simple but effective system for quickly deciding if a job is worth taking, or if it will be more trouble than it is worth.

Technique #2: Do It Right

Another problem-customer-filtration management trick that
saves me an awful lot of trouble is the simple insistence on
doing the job absolutely according to code and proper
procedure.

The problem to avoid here is not so benign as someone who
just wants to save a little money by cutting a corner. That is
logical and rational and I can understand it. The problem here
is, it's an odd phenomenon of human nature than some people
simply cannot allow themselves to do anything correctly.

It's not about price. Doing the proper solution, like maybe
using the proper gauge of wire or the proper wattage of bulb,
could cost the same, or even less, but some people have this
odd embedded bug of self destruction. They compulsively
choose to do it all wrong.

(At this point, dear reader, you may be thinking I am some
sort of wacky eccentric, having delusions about, or overly
sensitive reactions to, other people's behavior. Well let me
tell you this: I was once like you. I used to listen to trade and
service people talk about how insane some of their customers
could be; like you, I thought it was all wacky, paranoid,
delusional nonsense. Then I learned. Some people are just

nuts.)

One theory of why insisting on doing it correctly filters out problem customers is, you're essentially saying, "I do not wish to participate in your staged drama."

One sure way to get yourself tangled up into a stranger's staged drama is to participate in creating a situation where something is likely to break and cause harm. When it inevitably breaks, they will cast you, dear friend, as the villain. This gives them someone to blame for their troubles other than themselves, and provides an outlet for all their festering ire.

There is always a temptation to do what seems to be a quick simple band-aid-on-a-leper task for a quick buck, but there is an unwritten rule in the home repair biz, that "once you touch it, you own it." Something could have already been broken 16 different ways before you ever showed up, but once you touch it, everything that goes wrong with that lock or staircase or faucet can now be arguably attributed to you and what YOU did.

Incidentally, this kind of client is yet another reason why I can never do handyman work through some centralized go-between aggregator. There is too much variation, not just from job to job, but from customer to customer. To be effective as a handyman, you have to treat each customer as a unique entity, otherwise you start to not listen, and in handymanning, that is death. Plus, every house has a history of good or bad repairs, and all of that has to be taken into account.

Technique #3: Avoid the S**t Shows

Another thing to watch out for is a house that is labeled in the biz as a "s**t show." This refers to a house that has multiple layers of problems beyond or beneath the obvious one you have been called to address.

For example, maybe they just want you to do a simple patch on the vinyl siding. You charge in, but then you discover that your nail won't hold the patch piece because the stud underneath has been eaten by termites. But even if you replace that, you then discover that the replacement of the stud has disturbed asbestos-laden insulation, so now you are responsible for a hazmat remediation. Even if you do that too, you then discover that the foundation is cracked. It never ends. It's a s**t show. And it's not an accident. It did not happen overnight. These conditions are created by a certain type of person, over years and years.

This client psychology aspect of the work is, in and of itself, rather fascinating, as when you get down to business with another human being and the actual spending of money is about to occur, people take off much of their normal daily mask and tell you much about their true inner selves. In some cases, much of what they mask over is not very pretty. If you are into this sort of thing, you get a fabulous vantage point for observing the human condition.

Technique #4: Gig Teases

One category of problem client that is fairly easy to spot is the type of client I call a "gig tease."

It goes more or less like this: A new customer will call and say, "I am buying a new house in a few months, and I am planning to hire you to do as much work on it as you are willing to do. I am just waiting on the bank paperwork."

Gosh, the heart leaps with visions of cash galore. Then they say:

We can't get going on anything big until after the closing of course, but if you want to get started, I just dropped my keys into the cesspool in the back yard. I need you to come fish them out, and I can pay you $5."

If you are a newbie in the business, it's easy to fall into this trap. The initial vision of economic happily ever after sounds so great you may lose sight of reality, which in this case is wading into a cesspool for $5, and nothing else.

This kind of customer is actually not consciously trying to manipulate you. They just think they have to inflate the amount of business they may offer, because otherwise you would not like them or accept them. Kinda sad, really.

Technique #5: There Are No Small Jobs

Another common experience in the realm of handymanning is customers who are in denial over the extent or severity of a problem. A major alarm should always go off in your head whenever a customer uses the word "small" when describing their issue.

It's actually something of a major giveaway when someone uses the word "small." If someone wants me to move a "small" window air conditioner, that tells me the air conditioner is small relative to the HVAC system in the Empire State building, but I'm also willing to bet that it's too big for one guy to carry up a flight of stairs. When someone says they have a "small" hole in a ceiling, all that tells me is that it's probably less than 50% of the surface area of the entire room, so, it might be 200 square feet. I much prefer to hear that someone just has a hole in their ceiling. If they say that, I know it's a nifty small little hole. If they go out of their way to describe it as a small hole, I know it's eight feet across.

The main point I wish to make here is, it's a very common human shortcoming to want to close one's eyes to bad news. When someone calls you with a problem, of course they want to minimize the scope of the task, and make themselves believe that this will be a simple painless fix for the smallest amount of money possible. That's understandable. But every time someone calls you to come over and do a "small" job, you have to always be on the alert. When they feel the need to call it "small," that's because it probably isn't, and their "small" problem is often a symptom of a much larger problem, which has grown even larger because of an ongoing desire to close eyes to the full depth of the problem.

Technique #6: Walking Away

Another classic phrase in the trades: "You make the most money from the jobs you walk away from."

This bizarre turn of phrase teaches you to avoid jobs that might hook you into all kinds of unpaid remedial work. While excessive amounts of work may sound like job security, you generally want to avoid doing any kind of fix that has no clear end game in sight.

Remember, "Once you touch it, you own it," so if you sense uncertainty as to whether or not the job at hand can be brought to a quick conclusion, as opposed to the horrific possibility that once you rip up one board you will have to rip up 50, you learn to walk away.

This rule is somewhat similar to the rule regarding the avoidance of "s**t shows." However, it also applies to jobs that are not s**t shows per se, but are simply beyond your current level of skills, tools, and experience.

By not getting into a situation where you would end up having to work for free for multiple hours to stabilize a disaster area exposed by your well-intended attempt to do a small fix, (or spending multiple hours learning a new skill that is rarely called for) , you now have free time that you can sell elsewhere.

That's how you make the most money from jobs you walk away from.

Technique #7: Cultivate Good Clients

Most people–90% at least–are nice, kind, generous, sincere, easy to work with folks. It's only about 10% that are compulsively problem and misery creating. The real challenge is to not let that 10% take up all of your time or determine your customer service policies.

Just one example: I used to have a company do jobs for me, and I had paid them thousands of dollars over the years. One day I was short on cash and I needed to charge my entire order on a credit card. The owner said, "I'm sorry, but years ago I had a customer who charged his entire order on a credit card. He wasn't happy, and the credit card company made me refund all the money back to him. So now it's my company policy: it's a minimum 50% cash up front on your order or no deal." I pleaded, I cajoled, I pointed out how much business I had given him in the past, but all was for naught.

I hope you can see the mistake this guy made–he had encountered one crooked jerk, and now he treated ALL of his customers like they MIGHT be crooked jerks.

Since I was clearly not special to him, he was no longer special to me. He lost my loyalty. He jostled me out of my somnambulant state of just calling him by default. I started to look around, and found another, cheaper, better vendor. In saving himself from a possible loss, he created a definite loss of all my business, now and forever, amen.

If you create this kind of overly self-protective negative energy, the lousy customers might stick with you because no one else wants them, but the good ones will drift away because your energy does not feel right to them.

I was amazed to discover the degree to which handymanning is very much a relationship business. When I started, I presumed that I would work for a different stranger every day, but instead, it has become very much like a medical practice. If people like you and trust you, they will hire you repeatedly for all kinds of work. After a while, you don't even need to advertise, and you don't want to, because you don't want to be out where the 10% can find you.

Technique # 8: Don't Chase the Rabbit

One of the biggest changes in consciousness that comes with doing handyman work has to do with the sheer volume of work. It is a true tectonic shift

In every other career I had before handymanning, I was endlessly dogged by a less than full schedule. I was always concerned about hustling up more work by promoting myself.

But in this brave new world of tools and boots, while there may be a slow week here and there, for the most part, if you are a decent plumber or electrician or plaster guy, you no longer live in that world of scarcity. Work just flows in constantly. Sometimes it floods.

Even though the phone keeps ringing, it is very easy to remain in the old panicked fear mode, and run out on Saturdays and take every job. But the fact is, you can never, never, ever, finish. You need to rest. Most jobs are not true emergencies. It's Friday, it's 4 o'clock. Sit down, have a beer, and turn off your phone. There will be more calls Monday. Don't chase the rabbit.

The Handyman Whisperer

I have often pondered the notion of giving presentations to average homeowners on how to talk to a handyman . . . or a plumber or an electrician for that matter. It never ceases to amaze me how people who are intelligent enough to at least collect the financial resources needed to own a home, often seem to be confused by this form of communication. It's a conceptual / cultural barrier that many people cannot seem to cross.

There are millions of people who do home repair work, and I dare not presume to speak for any of them except myself. But for what it is worth, here are a few common pitfalls that I would encourage you to avoid:

Handymanning is very much a consulting business, and as one mentor once told me, the three most important things about consulting are the relationship, the relationship, and the relationship. A handyman is very much like a primary care physician for your house. Just like your PCP you want to have a relationship with someone you like and trust. There are other philosophies of hiring handymen I suppose, but if you subscribe to my idea that you should build a relationship with your handyman, here are a few common pitfalls to avoid:

To begin, when you first contact me, I would advise you to never tell me a story of how your last handyman (or electrician or plumber) is no longer returning your calls. Yes, from your perspective, that guy was an irresponsible unprofessional jerk who didn't finish the job and abandoned you in your hour of need. Yes, it's mathematically possible that you were an innocent victim and he was a shiftless incorrigible bum.

On the other hand, I have to wonder: did he dump you because he had a good reason to do so?

Talking to me about how another service person has left you in lurch is a little bit like calling a girl for a first date, and starting the conversation by saying, "The last girl I dated dumped me for no apparent reason."

We all want to take your side, but . . . one cannot help but wonder what her motivations may have been. Best that you not mention her at all.

Next, one of the biggest mistakes callers make is starting the conversation with the question, "How much do you charge?" Oy.

Talking about prices before we have even discussed the job or even gotten acquainted causes two problems: One, if money is your #1 issue, I have to wonder if you can afford to pay me at all. But what is far worse about that question is, it is an insult to the handyman spirit. It implies that you think a service person like me is a generic nameless commodity. On a deeper level, it leads me think that you think of *yourself* as a generic nameless commodity.

Hiring a skilled tradesperson is not like buying a commodity service. It's more like hiring a sculptor or a violinist. The money is a very small part of the "price." If the money is all you care about, alas, you will likely get a guy who only cares about the money as well, not about you or your house.

Note, if you are truly broke, or you are student or whatever, it's perfectly okay to say (later in the conversation, after we have gotten to know each other a little) that you are down on your luck these days and you are hoping to do this job as economically as possible. As long as you are being honest and not insulting me, I can work with that. There are always the good-better-best items in paints and everything else, and there are patches that are not ideal but will work for a year. Let me be the hero in solving your problem, not the villain.

(Incidentally, all of this advice works in reverse; I often have people call up who exude such exceptional personal generosity and wealth of spirit that they make me want to drop everyone else and come take care of them right away. I am just focusing on the negative end here, because those ultra-positive-energy folks need no "people skills" help from me.)

Oh, and just a pet peeve of my own: never leave messages for three different handymen and then hire the first one who calls you back. Imagine for a moment calling three girls for a date and only taking out the one who calls you back first. How do you think the other two will feel about, and react to, calls from you in the future? Again, if you treat people like commodities, the results are seldom optimal.

Please do remember, when hiring a tradesperson to fix your home, they will be entering your personal space. You may be asking them to descend into a nasty, dirty, spider-infested crawl space, or perhaps brave a rickety ladder to go up into a cramped hot attic. Once they get down or up there, you are asking them to deal directly with the oh-so-unforgiving laws of physics on your behalf, all the while not doing anything that might damage your home or put you in danger of injury or even death. This deserves your respect.

Apotheosis, or, Classism 101

Much as I hate doing this, I have to admit to being something
of a classist. Given how I was systematically trained to think
this way, it would be surprising if I was not.

This training in classism started early. Every year in my
elementary school, all the kids my age were divided into
"classes" of about 25 kids each, and it was understood that the
kids in class A were somehow "better" than the kids in class
B. Since I was safely ensconced in class A, I was in total
agreement with this arrangement, and saw no reason to
question it.

This academic apartheid became ever more apparent in 9th
grade, when those of us who were obedient to the teachers and
good at clerical work were placed in "college prep" courses.
We studied postmodernist philosophy whilst the "lower grade
people" were sent to woodshop classes.

Even at the time, I recall thinking, "Gee, I would kinda like to
learn how to weld, seems like a useful skill to have," but I was
shunted away from it, with a silent but nonetheless powerful
admonishment: as an "A grade student," it was somehow
"beneath me" to be in a class of "slow learners" and acquire
that sort of work-with-your-hands menial labor skill. It was

pure shame with no logic, but it was effective on me nevertheless.

When pundits and politicians comment on the woefully divided nature of our society, I am always curious as to why they do not talk about how our society is systematically divided in our education system. In my own experience, we were all classified as being grade A, B, C, D or F students, just like one classifies eggs or beef carcasses. The popular culture and society in general idealize the kids who go to college, and portray people in the trades as second tier.

Why are we then so very surprised, when this cultural division between white and blue collar kids results in their being tribally polarized as adults? The genesis of this social division is all the more obvious when you consider the extreme differences in experience for the A-B tribe vs. the C-D-F tribe. For the A-B kids, school is fun, and a path to rewards, membership, and promotion; for C-D-F kids, school is a boring grind, and a constant state of being told you are stupid. And of course, there is the ongoing patronizing attitude of the AB's towards the CDF's, which leads to the cumulative effect of creating envy, resentment, and mutual contempt. As a society, we are not victims here; this is a paradigm of our own making.

After all that social conditioning of school, fast forward 40 years, where, in the wake of the dreadnaught of the great recession, I found myself having that common yet oh so unappealing status of being both over 50 and "over qualified." My membership in the cum laude society and $4 would get me a cup of coffee at Starbucks, and I didn't have $4. Nearing my wit's end trying to find "knowledge work," my sister said, "You have always been good at fixing things, why don't you work as a handyman?"

At this point I found myself looking squarely at my own classist attitudes. Yes, I was good at fixing things, and I genuinely enjoyed doing it, but oh my goodness, what would people think of me, if I were to do this "lower class" kind of work? "What a horrific demotion in social standing," I thought.

Well, the universe moves in mysterious ways, and from day one I found myself being too busy making money as a handyman to think too much about it. Still, when I had moments to reflect, it bothered me a lot. And it took me over a year to come to terms with it.

My conclusion was a broad epiphany bordering on shock. I was thoroughly amazed, for someone who had always been labeled as being so "smart," at how far I had been suckered into embracing a world view that was not just evil, but also totally baseless and incorrect.

I had been led to believe that people who do "knowledge work" are somehow better, thus more deserving, than people who do work requiring use of their hands in the physical realm. Sad to say, this dogma, while commonly promulgated, falls apart under the slightest scrutiny.

Take, for example, the aphorism that "college graduates make more money than non-college graduates." Yes, this is probably true if you include everyone, including the trust fund heirs on the college side and the incarcerated felons and quadriplegics on the other. But if you adjust the numbers and compare the *average* college graduate to the *average* person who is motivated to work and goes into the trades, you will find the numbers invert. The average college graduate, especially if you include those who major in English, music, art history, education, and philosophy, generally makes far less than the average motivated-to-work plumber, plaster guy, bricklayer, HVAC tech, locksmith, or electrician. In fact, if you look closely, you may find that the average plumber makes more over the course of his working lifetime than a primary care physician. And let's face it, plumbers and proctologists are essentially in the same business.

There is a very practical issue needing to be addressed here, which is, we are endlessly short of skilled labor in the trades. This can have an invisible but powerful effect on the overall economy. Building a factory might be a great idea, but if there aren't enough welders available to build it, you're stuck. I will echo Mike Rowe and Peter Thiel here and reiterate the fact that we don't need everyone to go to college. As a modern industrial society we cannot function without plumbers, welders, plaster guys, and electricians. Liberal arts studies are fine for some folks, but I feel compelled to remind you, dear reader, that all the postmodernist thought in the world will not fix your broken toilet.

If we endlessly imply to our younger generations that any path other than college is a lesser life, if we continue to disregard the simple math of what skills the market is willing to pay for, if the popular culture continues to glorify higher education and conditions us to think of mechanics and HVAC guys as people who have failed in life, we will endlessly struggle to maintain our gas pipes and bridges. We also risk creating a management class that has little hands-on experience, leading to a baseless thus fragile sense of entitlement. This never ends well.

If you want to go solar, that means someone has to climb up on a hot roof and install those panels. The more you disincentivize people to do that kind of work, the more expensive it gets–if you can find someone to do it at all.

There is a broader problem that comes of this classist thinking: if you have one group of citizens tracked at an early age into abstract knowledge work, and another group of citizens that is brought up to deal with the unforgiving harsh physical reality of building and maintaining infrastructure, inevitably, even without the usual classist overlay, those two groups will culturally, linguistically, and politically diverge.

Republics always die of factionalism. Language consists of the labels we put on experience, and if respective experiences diverge too far, a cultural and political rift will inevitably follow. One of the primary goals in creating our public school system with its compulsory attendance was to take a disparate population of immigrants and native peoples, and meld them into an *unum* from the *pluribus*. Too much cultural difference between knowledge work and boots/blue jeans work is creating a dangerous divide, one that our forefathers knew had to be addressed in building a cohesive nation.

When I started doing handyman work, I was worried that my friends might no longer accept me if I stopped doing glamourous white collar work. Well, a little inside tip for you: once word gets out that you know how to fix broken windows and caulk a sink, you will never be lonely.

And while I was under the initial impression that I would be doing unappealing work, work that no one in their right mind would choose to do if they could do privileged knowledge work in a cubicle for 60 hours a week, I kept noticing that I had more and more choices. Because the demand for my services has been non stop, I work doing what I want, when I want, for whom I want. I get paid on the spot. I also get to dress very comfortably. The work is never boring. And as long as people choose to live in houses, I have permanent job security.

In sum, it is astonishing that such a high level of freedom would be classified by some as being a lower level of existence.

All I can say is, don't knock it 'til you've tried it.

Justin Locke, dba "Justin the Handyman," does basic handyman work in Metrowest Boston. Visit his blog at

justinlocke.com/Justin_the_Handyman2/

Send email to:

handyauthor@gmail.com

CPSIA information can be obtained
at www.ICGtesting.com
Printed in the USA
BVHW031259180422
634615BV00005B/12